ISBN 978-1-330-91801-2
PIBN 10121253

For support please visit www.forgottenbooks.com

1 MONTH OF
FREE
READING

at

www.ForgottenBooks.com

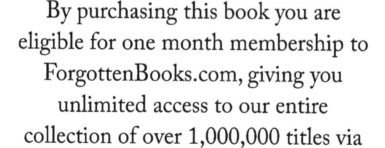

By purchasing this book you are
eligible for one month membership to
ForgottenBooks.com, giving you
unlimited access to our entire
collection of over 1,000,000 titles via
our web site and mobile apps.

To claim your free month visit:

www.forgottenbooks.com/free121253

English
Français
Deutsche
Italiano
Español
Português

www.forgottenbooks.com

Mythology Photography **Fiction**
Fishing Christianity **Art** Cooking
Essays Buddhism Freemasonry
Medicine **Biology** Music **Ancient**
Egypt Evolution Carpentry Physics
Dance Geology **Mathematics** Fitness
Shakespeare **Folklore** Yoga Marketing
Confidence Immortality Biographies
Poetry **Psychology** Witchcraft
Electronics Chemistry History **Law**
Accounting **Philosophy** Anthropology
Alchemy Drama Quantum Mechanics
Atheism Sexual Health **Ancient History**
Entrepreneurship Languages Sport
Paleontology Needlework Islam
Metaphysics Investment Archaeology
Parenting Statistics Criminology
Motivational

OVERPRESSURE

IN HIGH SCHOOLS IN DENMARK

OVERPRESSURE

IN

HIGH SCHOOLS IN DENMARK

BY

DR. HERTEL

MUNICIPAL MEDICAL OFFICER, COPENHAGEN

TRANSLATED FROM THE DANISH

By C. GODFREY SÖRENSON

WITH INTRODUCTION

By J. CRICHTON-BROWNE, M.D., LL.D., F.R.S.

London

MACMILLAN AND CO.

1885

Printed by R. & R. CLARK, *Edinburgh.*

CONTENTS.

a

INTRODUCTION.

DURING recent discussions on educational over-pressure in this country it has been repeatedly argued, and sometimes by those who ought to be well informed, that the complaints made must be exaggerated, because in other European countries, in which children of all classes are subjected to school work far more rigorous and protracted than any that is yet known with us, no murmur of dissatisfaction has been heard. Struck by this observation, and anxious to ascertain why it was that English children broke down at a point on the hill of knowledge which their Continental compeers surmounted with ease, I have been at some pains to inquire into the matter and have discovered that the observation is groundless, and the argument founded on it consequently worthless. The fact is, that in every country in North-Western Europe there have been, of late years, some popular agitation on the subject of educational overpressure and scientific protests against it and its attendant evils of a more or less emphatic character. In France, Germany, Switzerland, Denmark, Sweden, and Norway parents and physicians have given audible expression to their discontent with existing educational arrangements, and to their fear that the excessive and growing demands, made by schools upon the time and attention of children, will deteriorate the public health, while in several of these countries official inquiries have been held which have resulted in a demonstration of the existence of overpressure in certain directions.

One curious fact which has been brought to light in my survey of European countries with reference to overpressure is, that in every one of them in which the question has been raised, the international argument, if I may so call it, which set me forth on my survey, has been freely employed to silence those who have presumed to say that overpressure is no myth. Whenever in France, Germany, or elsewhere it has been suggested that the educational coach was being driven a little too fast, the prompt rejoinder has been that its rate of progress must be accelerated rather than slackened if the country is not to be left behind in the race of races, and that no complaints have been made about foreign coaches which go farther and faster. When Germans grumble that their children are over-worked, they are told that they must work harder still if industrial and commercial rivalry with England is to be maintained, and when Norwegians hint that the studies prescribed for their arts examination might be reasonably reduced, they are assured that the requirements of the Danish code are much higher than those of their own, and that in Denmark no objections have been made. A man of any patriotism or "self-respect of race," as Lord Rosebery has called it, is loath to admit that his own offspring are of feebler brain-fibre than those of his neighbour across the frontier, and so the comparisons instituted between the educational systems of different countries have materially helped to moderate the severity of the adverse criticism to which all of them have been subjected, and to bolster up the vicious elements which each of them contains. But these comparisons have been, in great degree, based on ignorance or misapprehension, and it has seemed to me very desirable that we, in England, should understand that the cry, which we have heard in our midst, against overpressure is not a mere outburst of insular spleen, but that the grievances and hurtful consequences included under that term have been clearly recognised in other countries. And thus it is, that I have undertaken to introduce to English readers Dr. Hertel's little work on *Overpressure in High Schools in Denmark.*

In selecting Dr. Hertel's monograph on overpressure for republication in this country, out of several on the same subject that have been sent to me, I have been influenced, partly by the circumstances that the original is in a language which makes it more inaccessible to English readers than French or German works, and that the ability and kindness of my friend Mr. Sörenson put a good translation of it within my reach, but principally by the conviction that it is an eminently careful and scientific treatise, and places in a clear light the dangers and difficulties which beset educational enterprise in the present day. No one can examine Dr. Hertel's tables without being satisfied that they are the fruit of much honest and laborious research, or study his conclusions without recognising that they are sound and irresistible, or weigh his recommendations without feeling that they are conceived in a spirit of extreme moderation. So temperate are his statements, so modest his demands, in view of revelations as to juvenile serfdom and pedagogic exactions, which might well warrant some warmth and drastic proposals, that no charge of professional bias or Utopian extravagance can possibly be brought against him. He who pleads for only half an hour, for a midday meal, out of a school session of six or seven hours' duration, who asks no more than nine hours' sleep in the twenty-four, for children ten years old, and who would be content, if boys of sixteen were not called on to apply themselves to brain work for more than ten hours a day, six days a week, can scarcely be said to be ultra-sanitarian in his notions or exorbitant in his requirements. Most English medical men and physiologists will hold that Hertel has formed far too high an estimate of the receptivity and power of endurance of nineteenth-century children, and that a far more liberal relaxation than he has adumbrated of the present school system in Denmark is imperatively needed if the Danes are to remain a vigorous and intelligent people.

Dr. Hertel's treatise, it will be noted, deals with overpressure exclusively as it exists in high schools, which are attended by the children of the affluent or well-to-do classes, and it may be thought, therefore, that it can have but little bearing on the controversy on that subject which has been going on here, and which has had reference to overpressure as it occurs in elementary schools, which are attended by the children of the humbler classes, of whom a considerable proportion are indigent or miserably poor. But overpressure, although it appears under different conditions and phases, is always very much one and the same thing; and an attentive study of it in any one of its spheres of operation is sure to facilitate the comprehension of it as a whole. Besides it must not be supposed that overpressure is confined to high schools in Denmark and elementary schools in England. Inquiries undertaken subsequently to the publication of Dr. Hertel's report have shown that the lower schools in Denmark are infested by it, and abundant evidence may be adduced that high schools in this country are not free from its baleful influence. In Denmark its incidence is more uniform in schools of different grades than it is in England, where in high schools it falls chiefly on the clever children, who are capable of being forced forward to win scholar-

ships or other distinctions, and in public elementary schools on the dull children, who must be
forced up to the examination level. And, no
doubt, there are differences in its consequences
corresponding to this difference of incidence, but
in both countries it affects similarly large numbers
of delicate children, who are taxed beyond their
strength and have to work under unhealthy conditions, and in both it induces on the large scale
the same kind of ailments. Dr. Hertel's observa-
tions will therefore be found instructive in relation
to overpressure in schools of all ranks, though, of
course, they are especially applicable in the case
of middle class day schools in this country.

It may be admitted at once that the state of
matters in Copenhagen, described by Dr. Hertel,
is far worse than anything that exists with us in
schools of the same class. As regards the hours
of school work, private study, and preparation
required of them, and the distribution of these
throughout the day, and the circumstances under
which they work, Danish children are obviously

placed at a disadvantage when compared with children in England. It seems probable that, owing to faulty guidance in infancy, there are in Denmark a larger proportion of children than in England who begin their school course in a state of debility or tainted with disease; while it is certain that throughout that course in Denmark the great body of children are deprived of invigorating exercise in the open air, and the exhilarating influence of games in a way that would not be tolerated here. But, on the other hand, it may be contended that English middle class children live, on the whole, in an atmosphere of greater excitement than do their contemporaries in Copenhagen, and that they are subjected, in far larger numbers, to the stimulus of competition and the worry of examination. " To provoke a boy," says Ruskin, "whatever he is, to want to be something better, and wherever he was born to think it a disgrace to die, is the most entirely and directly diabolic of all the countless stupidities into which the British nation has been of late betrayed by its avarice and irreligion." But this diabolic stupidity is, it must be admitted, very prevalent amongst us, and bids fair, if unchecked, to put us very shortly on a level with Denmark in respect of the sickliness of our rising generation. Year by year our children are driven into the struggle for existence at an earlier age ; new incentives are invented to goad or lure them to fierce efforts in the conflict, and greater stress is laid upon shabby intellectual tactics by which they may outwit their opponents. Competitive examination, feverish excitement, and cram are rampant amongst us, and these, if they have not yet afforded in our schools such a copious crop of degeneration and disease as Hertel has found in Copenhagen, have yet borne fruits that are plentiful and deplorable.

All the varieties of sickliness that Hertel has enumerated are to be found in our schools in this country of every class, though, of course, some of them abound more in schools of a particular order. Thus, scrofula is most prevalent in public element-ary schools, and no observant person can look round one of these in a poor district of a large town without being painfully impressed by the number of children presenting signs of its actual presence or the well-known characteristics of a predisposition to it, in their fine silky hair, transparent skin, delicate features, small bones, and narrow shoulders. Nervousness, on the other hand, is most prevalent in schools of a superior description, and perhaps finds its acme in an intense high school for girls, where all sorts of muscular twitchings and antics signalise the petty nerve-storms that eddy within, and that are liable any day to gather into a devastating cyclone of disease. But in schools of all classes representative cases of each of Hertel's groups are to be encountered, and the number of cases, belonging to certain groups, occurring in any school is often a fair index of the pitch to which overpressure pure and simple, or reinforced by other unfavourable hygienic conditions, has reached in it.

When it is alleged that overpressure prevails extensively in middle-class schools in this country no general censure is thereby necessarily implied on those engaged in the conduct of such schools. It is undoubtedly true that some schoolmasters and mistresses are so recklessly bent on serving their own interests, or are so possessed by the demon of education, that they are regardless of the health of their pupils, and culpably blind to the mischief they do. I heard lately of a lady teacher of much experience and with some pretensions to science who stated deliberately and with emphasis that it was impossible to over-work any girl, however hard you tried, and I thought I should have liked to have shown her two little girls who were under my observation at the time—one mad, the other coughing away her lungs—whose maladies were as clearly due to school work and worry as is smallpox to infection. But scholastic bigotry of this kind is comparatively rare, and the large majority of schoolmasters and mistresses are, it is believed, alive to the existence of overpressure, and anxious to do their best to avoid or mitigate it. Many of them, probably from the want of

physiological insight or from professional near-
sightedness, under-estimate its prevalence and
make too light of the dangers which attend it; but
a few, at any rate, fully appreciate its extent, and
deplore the part they are unwillingly compelled to
play in promoting it. Schoolmasters and mistresses
are not mainly responsible for overpressure. The
blame of it must be laid, in the final resort, on
the spirit of the age, on a false notion of the
value of life, on an erroneous conception of
the aim and office of instruction, and more immediately on the vanity and cupidity of parents.
Almost before a baby boy has left his cradle in these
days, and long before his capabilities can be known,
his career has often been marked out for him.
Throughout childhood it is constantly impressed
on him that his chief end in life is to win scholarships and prizes, or to make his way in this world
by the sweat of his brain. When he should still
be at home in happiness and contentment he is
sent off to a preparatory school, where some successful crammer with relentless grasp squeezes

him into the approved form for satisfying the requirements of certain examiners. And almost before he has got his permanent canine teeth he is involved in contest and emulation. The sweep of the past generation who held a lighted straw wisp to the feet of his apprentice to help him up a strait chimney was almost humane when compared with the father of the period, who plagues and goads his son for years together, and sometimes, even when his health is obviously failing, to force him through the narrow and crushing vent of some examination. It is undoubtedly true that foolish and greedy parents compel teachers to overpress very young boys, and that the seeds of suffering and incapacity are therefore sown in preparatory schools. Accurate information as to the health of boys in these schools is not yet procurable, but I have notes of two cases in which boys who had just emerged from such schools and won scholarships died of brain fever before they could enter on the enjoyment of them, and I have been told lately by a high authority on all educational questions a fact that perhaps reflects some light on what goes on in them. The fact is, according to my informant, that in one large public school it is the understood rule that no hard work is required for the first year of the scholars who have, it may be presumed, come from preparatory schools or been submitted to processes similar to those which are carried on in them. For twelve months these scholars are allowed to be comparatively idle in order that they may recover from the severe strain involved in winning their scholarships, and no physiologist will be in doubt whether their tremendous spurt and long rest or a quiet steady continuous pull would have carried these boys farther in the end.

It is not, of course, suggested that all preparatory schools are engaged in cramming, or that all of them lend themselves to overpressure even at the instigation of heartless or eager parents. On the contrary, it is well known that many of them perform with the utmost efficiency, discrimination, and forbearance the momentous work of grounding which devolves on them, and which might perhaps without exaggeration be said to be equal to about three-fifths of a boy's whole formal education. It is well known that many of them very jealously guard the health and foster the development of the children entrusted to them, but still they are all dominated to some extent by the presiding spirit of strife, vainglory, and emulation; and in many of them overpressure is strenuously applied.

In middle-class day schools, which correspond most closely with the schools in Copenhagen examined by Hertel, the extent to which over-pressure prevails cannot be accurately gauged any more than in the case of preparatory schools. But that it does prevail, and to no small degree in some of them, may be inferred from the observa-tions of medical men on the illnesses of boys attending them, from our knowledge of the work they carry on, and the results they attain, and from the complaints of parents. We hear frequently of headaches, nose-bleedings, anæmia, and other nervous affections in boys who are pupils in such schools. We hear constantly of the complaints of parents that their sons have to sit up till eleven or twelve at night to prepare their lessons, and must, if they are at all slow of acquisition, either have skilled assistance or lag hopelessly behind and be branded stupid. We know that these schools are engaged in the universal competition, and that they are controlled by examinations, which Mr. Pridgin Teale, in his statement to the General Medical Council, accompanying his visitation report, called "the tyrants of education." "Examinations," Mr. Pridgin Teale went on, and his words are entitled to great weight, for they were ordered to be printed by the Council, and are therefore in some degree backed by the authority of the Medical Parliament :—"Examinations have been and are not only potent for good, but I fear very often for evil. We who are practitioners are perpetually fighting the battle of poor over-worked young brains, allured by that *ignis fatuus* of prizes, scholarships, and university class lists. Examinations at the present time, whether in the universities, or still more in the competitions in civil and military life, are becoming one mighty force of which the result is expressed in their influence upon the brain and nervous system. The outcome of education,—training, is about the last thing that seems to be thought of by those who have the planning and the conduct of these examinations."

One outcome of education fevered by examination, which is perhaps not thought of but is certainly realised, is a vast amount of ill-health, and another outcome, which is anything but desired but very surely attained, is a vast amount of ignorance and stupidity. As in elementary schools clever children who would repay the pains spent upon them are left untended, in order that the dull ones, who are to a great extent ineducable, may receive special tuition, so in secondary schools boys of meagre or average ability who would particularly profit by assistance are sometimes woefully neglected in order that brilliant boys, who have reached a stage of mental evolution when they can very well help themselves, may be made still more brilliant, if happily they do not burn out prematurely, or are not quenched by some disease. It is truly astonishing to contemplate the sluggishness of intellect and poverty of information which numbers of boys exhibit after ten or twelve years of expensive schooling, and it is truly pitiful to observe the narrowness of mind and weakness of character which numbers of boys who have been accounted brilliant at school manifest when brought into contact with men and affairs. There are boys who have escaped any actual disease during a long course of overpressure, but who, after its final wave has carried them triumphantly over the last examination, are left stranded in a state of nervous exhaustion. Like young Toots, they seem to leave off having brains when they begin to have whiskers. They are listless and depressed, they seem to have lost that keen interest in life which every healthy young animal should feel. As they grow up they look on beauty with lack-lustre eye, hear the great voice of ocean with no heart-stirring, sniff the freshness of the spring with nothing but an apprehension of catarrh, and do not even smack their lips over an oyster. Verily, it was not by men of this sort that the British Empire was built up!

In the case of boys, a hothouse education, overpressure, and incessant examinations are bad enough; but in the case of girls, who are far more powerfully affected by emulation, these are still worse in their effects.

Why, it may be asked, should large numbers of girls be gratuitously subjected to all the tortures of competitive examination, to the hazardous thrill of success, or the disappointment of failure in a prizeless race? For girls who are to enter on teaching as a profession certificates of proficiency are doubtless necessary, but why should multitudes of girls, who have no prospect of having to work for their living or of entering upon any pursuit in which academic distinctions will be serviceable, undergo all the risks of protracted brain labour directed towards a competitive trial in subjects some of which can have no application to their future circumstances? Why, but simply to gratify their own self-conceit and progenital pride. It is, of course, said that local examinations, senior and junior, licentiateships in arts, and science certificates, induce girls to work who would otherwise be idle, and give steadiness and aim to the studies of all who prepare for them, but it may, I think, be questioned whether these have really promoted true culture, whether they have not often deranged the work of schools, and whether they have not tended sometimes to substitute brittle and paltry pinchbeck for "the pure and ductile gold of ancient womanhood." But however all that may be, it cannot, I am sure, be questioned that these ordeals for girls are injurious to health. They come, be it remembered, at a critical period of life, when the nerve-centres are peculiarly impressionable, while the preparation for them extends through those years, when Hertel, adopting the recommendation of Miss Zahle, has urged that the school work of girls should be materially lightened. Every physician of authority on the diseases of women who has approached this subject, in England or America, has made virtually the same claim with Hertel, for a reduction and careful regulation of brain labour in girls from thirteen to sixteen years of age, and many of them have pointed out in strong and memorable terms the mischief to the individual and to society which must result from a disregard of hygienic laws in the case of girls at this epoch of life. Quite recently Dr. Thorburn of Manchester and Dr. Keiller of Edinburgh have condemned boldly the attempt to educate boys and girls on the same lines, and the craze for forcing the latter through examinations which might perhaps in a double sense be said to yield only barren honour. These distinguished physicians have quoted from their own experience cases of numerous disorders and diseases that have, in their judgment, been clearly attributable to the misdirection of the education of girls. They have pointed to the increased prevalence of hysteria, neuralgia, and sick-headache amongst young women of the middle and upper classes, and have connected this with the way in which education is now pushed on without any regard to natural periodicity. And they have uttered a well-timed warning that as the girls of to-day are to be the mothers of the next generation, and as the mother plays a pre-potential part in the formation of the nervous systems of her sons, very serious consequences must be anticipated from perseverance in our present system of female education.

In my own more limited experience I have seen instances of almost all the disastrous results of the educational overpressure of girls which Drs. Thorburn and Keiller have enumerated, and I would wish now to direct attention to another of its calamitous effects, upon which they have not dwelt, and to which Hertel only indirectly alludes, but which has been brought prominently under my notice, I mean consumption or phthisis, which is, I feel confident, induced during and by secondary education in girls who would have remained free from it had they been content to be a little less learned.

There is a growing conviction amongst pathologists, founded on accumulating evidence, that consumption is directly due to a microbe or germ, but this view of the true nature of the disease does not exclude the influence of states of the nervous system in conducing to its development. Every one is aware that a large number of highly educated young men and women succumb to consumption. In a moiety of these the high education and consumption stand in no causal relation to each other, but have their common root in a state of nervous organisation which predisposes alike to great cerebral activity and pulmonary failure. But in the other moiety there are good grounds for believing that the exhaustion resulting from prolonged nervous excitement, together with the imperfect expansion of the lungs and impaired nutrition, which are almost inseparable from studious and sedentary habits in early life, have really invited the disease. And this invitation of consumption by nervous over-strain and studious habits is especially apt to prove efficacious in the case of young women at the period of secondary education, because they have then, owing to other conditions, a remarkable proclivity to the complaint. At all ages above thirty-five, men die of consumption in much larger proportion than women; the rate for England and Wales calculated on a period of twenty years (1861-80) per million living was 3535 for the one and 2613 for the other. From twenty to thirty-five years of age the death-rate from this disease for the two sexes is almost equal, thus from 1861-80 it was per million living 3688 for men and 3748 for women. But from five to twenty years of age a very different state of matters is met with, for then the death-rate of females from consumption is vastly in excess of that of males. In the twenty years from 1861-80 the death-rate from consumption of males from fifteen to twenty years of age was 924 per million living, while that of females from fifteen to twenty years of age was 2740, and in males again from five to fifteen years of age it was 459 and in females 669. In infants under five years of age the male death-rate again preponderates.

Now in this enormously enhanced liability of females from five to twenty years of age to consumption, when compared with males, which I do not remember to have seen previously noticed, we have a clear indication of the necessity of avoiding every condition and habit of life that can possibly contribute to the establishment of the disease, and the corollary of this is that we should curtail rather than extend studious application, and insist on far more outdoor exercise for girls than they have hitherto enjoyed.

That the neglect of these indications up to this time, and the spread of the higher education of girls, have had some influence in causing consumption is, I think, suggested even by the Registrar-General's returns. Consumption has, of course, been greatly restricted in its ravages by sanitary reforms, and the death-rate from it has been falling steadily at all ages during the last twenty years. But, curiously enough, girls from five to fifteen years of age—who ought, one would have thought, considering their indoor life, to have benefited by these reforms more than boys—have really benefited by them less. The death-rate has in their case fallen considerably less than that of boys, and during the last five years it has actually ceased to fall, and has indeed risen slightly.

But other than statistical evidence is available to establish the connection between nervous overstrain and pulmonary consumption, for there are few medical men who cannot adduce cases which have come under their own observation of girls of exceptional ability and industry who have fallen victims to this malady, and who have certainly exposed themselves to its onslaughts by their devotion to their books. A typical case of the kind was that of Ellen Watson, the story of whose pure and spiritual life which coruscated from first to last with vivid intellectual light has been lately published. This gifted woman, who greatly distinguished herself at University College, and attained to a proficiency in mathematics which the late Professor Clifford (himself, by the way, a victim of consumption induced by inordinate mental activity) declared would have been remarkable in a man, died of consumption at the age of twenty-four. Her biographer distinctly states that Ellen Watson's fatal illness was not brought on by overstrain of mental work, but her narrative discredits her assertion. It may have been that Ellen Watson was constitutionally predisposed to consumption, of which indeed other members of her family have died, but every medical man will find in the history of the merciless intellectual discipline which she imposed on herself, in her incessant and strenuous exertions towards advancement, in the double strain on her energies in studying and teaching, and in her speculative anxieties sufficient to account for the incursion and rapid progress of lung decay, even in the absence of hereditary taint. Almost any young woman of nervous temperament put through the same toil and training would break down in the same way.

I have mentioned as contributory to the invasion of phthisis in over-educated girls a failure of general nutrition, but this in its turn may be attributable to educational overpressure. It is not only amongst the children of the half-starved poor that innutrition and poverty of blood interfere with brain function. Both categories of Burns's grace must be borne in mind :—

> "Some hae meat and canna eat,
>   And some wad eat that want it."

Besides the child that suffers from overpressure because its pinched brain lacks nutriment owing to an empty larder—the child that "wad eat but wants it," we have the child whose brain lacks nutriment because it is overpressed, and is thus bereft of appetite—the child that has "meat but canna eat." There are unquestionably many children belonging to the affluent classes in this country who are underfed because they are overpressed.

They have certainly more wholesome and digestible
viands provided for them than the portly sandwiches,
which all travellers in Denmark are familiar with,
and which constitute, according to Hertel, the sole
food of the children there until their late afternoon
dinner. But they are without appetite to partake
of the tempting comestibles that are placed before
them. As the school term goes on, they cease to
relish the meals which were so acceptable to them
during the holidays, and as the examination
approaches, they have sometimes a positive aver-
sion to solid food. Breakfast is the chief difficulty,
for it is especially characteristic of brain irritation
that it creates distaste for the morning meal. Out
of a broken and unrefreshing sleep haunted by
arithmetical dreams the overpressed child wakes
weary. The light which comes "stealing in at
morn" and should find it jubilant brings only a
sense of fatigue and disinclination to face the
trials of the day. But the recollection of evening
tasks soon drives away lethargy. After a hurried
toilet and perhaps a neglected bath the child comes

downstairs, pale and ill at ease, and with no relish for rolls. It toys with its food, pushes away its plate, drinks greedily a cup of tea, the neurotic properties of which it has already discovered, and then hastens off to school. There is a Scotch apothegm that a man who makes a good breakfast needs no certificate to moral character, and with more truth it may be said that the child who makes no breakfast needs no certificate to bad health. It may be laid down as a sound and universal rule that no brain work should be done by a child on an empty stomach. Buns or sandwiches at eleven o'clock will not make up for the want of a substantial breakfast. If, as has been alleged, a certain proportion of children of the affluent classes, and especially high-school girls, do go to school frequently without breakfast, or after only an apology for one, that fact may be received as at once a cause and an evidence of overpressure. For the brain, served with poor thin blood, cannot exert itself vigorously without detriment, and the absence of healthy appetite in a growing school child is a sign of cerebral exhaustion or irritation, or of a state of body in which that rapid and well-balanced destruction and construction of tissue which is essential to vigorous health has been seriously disturbed.

That the whole question of overpressure is deserving of anxious consideration no one who looks at it in connection with the tendencies of the age will for a moment doubt. Dr. James Ross of Manchester, one of the most able and philosophical physicians of the day, has just told us in his great work on the nervous system that psychical disturbances are likely to exercise a more and more predominant influence in the production of disease as civilisation advances. "The keen competition," he writes, "evoked by the struggle for existence in the higher departments of social life must subject the latest evolved portions of the nervous system to a strain so great that only those possessing the best balanced and strongest nervous systems can escape unscathed." The same thought has presented itself to Mr. Gladstone's comprehensive mind, for he

said some years ago: "The constantly-growing complexity of life appears to bring with it a constantly
growing complexity of disease. The pace at which
we live is quickened, the demands both on thought
and emotion are heightened without any corresponding increase of force in the organs or faculties
which are to meet these demands." Now, if this
be so, if modern life is to make ever-increasing
calls on the energies of our race, if disease is to
increase in complexity, and is to depend more and
more on psychical disturbances, it is clearly our duty
to provide, as far as may be, against the dangers
ahead by strengthening and husbanding the powers
of resistance of the young. There is no better
preparation for a stormy life than a tranquil and
happy childhood, and sound policy should guide
us to postpone as long as possible the entrance of
our children on that struggle in which so much is
to be required of them. But instead of obeying
the dictates of sound policy we do exactly the
reverse. We "flush to anticipate the scene." We
force back the struggle for existence into our

schools, abbreviate to the utmost that period of entire dependence on parental support which is the very measure of altitude in the scale of being, and lose not an instant in plunging our children into the vortex of nervous excitement. Instead of holding back, we spur on; instead of labouring steadily to build up a strong stable brain, we are content to hurry up one specious-looking externally, but radically rickety and infirm.

The brain, it should never be forgotten, is made up of explosive material, the explosiveness of which may be heightened or reduced. In states of disease such as insanity or epilepsy the brain-substance, or certain tracts of it, are raised to a higher degree of explosiveness, as gunpowder is when mixed with nitro-glycerine. In states of idiocy or imbecility it is reduced to a lower degree of explosiveness, as gunpowder is when mixed with moistened clay, so that it only burns slowly away or will not light at all. The discharge from healthy brain-substance, like the explosion of gunpowder, follows the lines of least resistance,—that is to say, the lines of customary functional activity ; but the discharge of unstable or unhealthy brain-substance is, like the explosion of dynamite, in too great a hurry to discriminate, and operates with extreme violence in all directions, thus causing unusual and confused combinations of action. The difference in action between a stable and healthy or unstable and unhealthy nerve-centre is analogous to that between a steady propulsion and a sudden blow. And this difference in action is dependent on a difference in chemical constitution analogous to the difference between gunpowder and dynamite. The substitution of an atom of one kind for an atom of another, or a rearrangement of atoms, makes all the difference. Now the differences in constitution between gunpowder and dynamite and their cognate nitrogenous compounds are determined in the processes of manufacture, and so the differences in constitution of nerve-centres are determined in the processes of their making or building up. It is manufacture that determines the result in the one case and nutrition in the other, and as an artificer presides over manufacture and regulates it, so functional activity presides over nutrition and regulates it. The artificer has the streams of commerce from which to select his materials, and functional activity has the currents of the blood from which to select its. And as the artificer is influenced by antecedent resolutions in his selection of materials, choosing saltpetre and carbon if he desires to produce gunpowder, and sulphuric acid and glycerine if he aims at nitro-glycerine, so functional activity is influenced by antecedent conditions in its calls on the blood, gathering in more or less nitrogen to construct more or less stable nerve-centres as these prescribe. And these antecedent conditions may be summed up under inherited predisposition, toxic agents, and abusive employment. From birth, or at some particular stage of growth, a nerve-centre may assume an explosive condition by virtue of some tendency bound up in its constitution. At any period of life its nutrition may be so interfered with by the action of poisonous agents like alcohol or strychnia that it becomes explosive temporarily or permanently. And at any period of life, but particularly at the great epochs of development, it may be so over-stimulated or exhausted by excessive or unsuitable work that mal-nutrition is established, with the train of explosive phenomena that depend on it. It is through the mal-nutrition of the higher nerve-centres which it sets up that educational overpressure induces the nervous disorders for which it is responsible, explosive disorders of unstable equilibrium, such as epilepsy, St. Vitus's dance, and sick headache. But education without overpressure—education in which hereditary restrictions, the laws of growth, the constitution of the organism, the vivifying power of happiness, and the paralysing effects of fear and rivalry are held constantly in view—may be made subservient to the better nutrition of all the nerve-centres, and brace and strengthen them to encounter without risk the trials that are in store for them. Education without overpressure—true education—is a supreme want of our time. Hertel has, I think, done something toward freeing education from overpressure, and therefore to promote true education by revealing the magnitude of the evil in his native country.

J. CRICHTON-BROWNE.

London, *June 1885.*

OVERPRESSURE

IN

HIGH SCHOOLS IN DENMARK.

CHAPTER I.

THE METHOD OF INQUIRY.

In few departments of knowledge has the universal progress which characterises the present time been so considerable as in all matters relating to hygiene. All classes are gradually awakening to the truth that prevention is better than cure. Great strides have also been made with regard to schools in the matter of hygiene in recent times; indeed, any improvements in this direction which have been achieved date back only thirty or forty years. In all civilised countries much more attention is now paid to physical development than formerly, and the school itself recognises the duty of uniting the intellectual with the physical

culture of the child entrusted to its care in such
a manner as to secure well-balanced development. It appears, however, that the schools of
the present day have not been very successful
in this twofold duty, for not only in Denmark
but from Sweden and Germany—to take only
our next-door neighbours—voices have been
heard loudly protesting that, while the child's
brain is being overtaxed, its bodily development
is being proportionately neglected, and that in
consequence the rising generation is becoming
more and more characterless and sickly. Thus
Professor Kjelberg of Upsala says :—" Overpressure has long existed in schools of all classes, and
the close observer has no difficulty in detecting
the results in the present generation. It is a common complaint that true power of mind and force
of character are wanting among the young men of
the present day." Dr. Kjelberg issues, therefore, a
strong warning against the overpressure existing in
schools, which restricts our youth to an unnaturally
sedentary life. In Germany, too, a lively controversy on this point is going on, and schoolmasters as well as doctors maintain with great

emphasis that too much is demanded from the young. As many will remember, the same complaints have resounded in Denmark from time to time, and notably in 1860 a hot contest was waged on the subject. Mr. C. Fog, headmaster of the Metropolitan School, and several other writers, in a number of treatises, directed powerful attacks against the system of teaching pursued in our classical schools, and especially against the number of subjects required to be got up in too short a time and under too great a pressure. The pupils, they alleged, did not thereby receive a sound and effective education, but left school worn out, dull, and destitute of mental energy. These writers drew their evidence mainly from their own experience as teachers, and Fog showed by statements and figures, bearing upon the time-table at the Metropolitan School, that nine to ten hours of daily work were very common among the pupils of the higher classes, while only a small number of pupils finished the school course in the normal time. Opposed to these practical teachers was chiefly Madvig, then inspector of schools, who also sought support for his opinions from his large personal experience. He denied that overpressure existed in general, though admitting the possibility of it in the second and third highest classes, if the teacher did not give particular attention to prevent it. Neither side gave detailed information as to the health of the children, or the amount of work actually done by them. It would appear, however, as if the matter was not satisfactorily disposed of, for in 1871 a new system was introduced, dividing the upper school into two sections, in one of which special attention was devoted to languages and history, while mathematics and science formed the principal subjects in the other; nevertheless, it is somewhat doubtful if this arrangement has afforded any real relief.

Amongst the most important contributions to the subject tendered by the medical faculty may be mentioned Professor Hornemann's treatise on *The Culture of Health and the Schools,* and one or two pamphlets by Professor Drachmann on girls' schools. The state of health in general in our schools has naturally been the principal subject dealt with by these writers, but, in particular, the hours of work are mentioned as a chief-cause of bad health among children. Several other writers, especially of late years, have also contributed articles to newspapers and periodicals, as well as in special pamphlets, on various questions connected with our subject.

The above short statement will suffice to show that complaints about the unsatisfactory condition of our schools have been heard at intervals for many years, and that they have not only proceeded from the medical faculty but also from the schools themselves. There are many, however, who still regard these complaints as unjustifiable, and the demands for an improved school hygiene as excessive, and these often employ an argument, to which they ascribe much weight, but which really is of no value. " Why," say they, " we, too, have been schoolboys under the present system, and we are nevertheless strong, healthy men, who have suffered no injury from our schooldays." It had been indeed deplorable if many had not escaped free of hurt from school, and that is so in our day as well ; but, apart from that, neither they who thus boast of their own

immunity from harm nor we who receive their
protestations with reserve know what was the
state of health in those days, for no one inquired
into the matter. It is none the less possible
that many have suffered from inordinate schooling in former days without having the slightest
suspicion that the school was the cause of their
weakness or ailments. Those who now give their
opinion on the state of health existing in schools
thirty or forty years ago were themselves schoolboys at the time, and I would ask if it can
really be thought that any schoolboy in our
own time could give a trustworthy answer if
asked about the state of health in his school.
I, for my part, would not ascribe any value to
such testimony. But, even supposing that the
general health in schools was comparatively good
forty years ago, that is no proof that such is
now the case. The present generation has quite
a different constitution from that of the last
one, when anæmia and nervousness (the chief
complaints of our time, and in particular of our
youth) were not nearly so widespread as they are
at present. This must be regarded as a perfectly

well-established fact, and is indeed generally admitted. It is therefore not without cause, nor owing to a merely artificial agitation, that improved hygienic conditions are now being so urgently demanded; they are actually required to a much greater extent than formerly.

We know as imperfectly now as we did forty years ago the true state of health among children, neither have we accurately ascertained how much they work. Each one judges only from his own experience and according to his own views on these points; the subjective opinion of the individual may be more or less correct, but it does not convince others. What we therefore require is a proof that there are in our schools many weak and sickly children, for whom good hygienic conditions are specially necessary; for, if the state of health in schools be good and satisfactory, as some masters and mistresses still believe, it would be absurd to demand improvements which are not absolutely needed, but which must necessarily entail an increased expenditure. So, too, it is necessary to know the hours of work in the different classes and for the different ages before discussing the question as to whether the time spent in work can be supposed to be injurious to the child's health and whole intellectual development. Nor can this question be disposed of entirely by the school authorities; it comes fully as much within the province of the doctor, the more so as no knowledge of the principles of health or of physiology is required of schoolmasters—in our country, at least; and one cannot, therefore, assume that they are qualified to judge of the health of the child. So many different factors have to be reckoned with on this point that it is often very difficult to determine how much influence each may exert. Let me remark here, therefore, that hard work is only one of them, although no doubt an important one. It would be preposterous to lay the whole responsibility for the weakness of the present generation upon the school, but it is certain that it ought to bear a large share of the blame.

The primary object of this essay, then, is to give a series of such detailed and methodically arranged facts as have never hitherto been brought forward,—firstly, as to the state of health in schools, because this must always be the principal factor in determining how far improved hygienic conditions are necessary ; and, secondly, as to the hours of work, and a few other matters, as far as I have been enabled to gain information under these heads.

My investigation has been confined to the better-class boys' and girls' schools in Copenhagen. I have not been able to extend it to the lower-class schools (though the state of health in the latter is far from satisfactory), partly because the task would have been far too stupendous, and partly because a different system of inquiry would have been necessary, owing to the greater difficulty in getting the parents of the humbler class children to give proper and reliable answers to questions. Even although there may have been children in the schools examined by me from smaller and poorer homes, still the great majority have belonged to the more affluent classes, so that we may reasonably assume that they enjoy all the advantages of healthy dwellings and sound nourishment. The materials I have collected may therefore be said to come from a pretty uniform source, and may be

trusted to give a fair idea of the state of health existing in the schools frequented by the children of the well-to-do population.

The manner in which I have tried to carry out my task is as follows : To each school I sent printed forms, having spaces to be filled in with information on the following points—the age and class of each pupil; the number of hours of school-work, and the time employed at home in preparation ; the amount of written exercises to be done at home; whether a private tutor aided the pupil in any branch, and, if so, for how many hours; whether the pupil had any difficulty on the whole, or in any particular subject; his state of health, the hour he went to bed, and how many hours' sleep he had; while a column was left for remarks by the teacher. The teacher was also requested to state whether the pupil in question was one of the best, middling, or dullest in his class as regards capacity ; all the other columns, with the exception of the first two, were to be filled up by the parents.

The demands thus made upon the parents were by no means inconsiderable, the answer being in many cases a matter of some difficulty, and it is therefore the more to be appreciated that the answers on the whole are clear and decided. I asked several headmasters what they thought of the answers returned to me, and they all replied that they considered them, on the whole, accurate and in accordance with their own knowledge of the children. Of course mistakes have arisen in a few cases, and here and there a column has been left unanswered, but I can state positively that such occurrences have been exceptional, and that the information given has been so complete and trustworthy that the result may reasonably be considered to be correct in the main. One column— that relating to the child's health—has, however, been comparatively often left blank, viz. in eight per cent of the total number of returns ; though, as most well-to-do people have a family doctor, who would have been willing to fill in the answer, it ought to have been easy to have supplied accurate information under that head. In several cases in which that column was left blank I know for certain that the children in question were unhealthy, and that the parents withheld the fact.

It is not easy to perceive a reason for this if the parents are willing to answer all the other questions. In several cases I fancy the reason was that the parents were in doubt as to the child's state of health; not being able to call it strong, they have nevertheless been unable to state that it was suffering from any particular disease, and have therefore given no answer at all. Later on I shall have occasion to show that the above is probably the true reason for particular information being withheld in certain cases. Not a few families refused all information whatever, some holding statistics to be misleading and delusive, and others regarding such inquiries in the light of an unjustifiable intrusion on their private family history.

It would have been satisfactory if those parents who had family doctors had entrusted them with the filling up of the column relating to health; in only 10 per cent of the cases has this been done, in all the others the parents having filled up the column themselves. This duty they have discharged on the whole, in a very clear manner, and in many cases a full description of the child's state of health has been given; the diagnosis would, however, have been more trustworthy had it been countersigned by the family doctor.

In spite of returns being withheld in many instances, the materials at hand are nevertheless so abundant that the result is only very slightly affected thereby. Where no answer at all has been given I have set the case down as "non-returned," and wherever an answer has exhibited dubiety or incoherency, or wherever the school authorities have signified that any particular answer may have been prompted by a misunderstanding, an entry has been made under the same heading.

The question as to whether the pupil found difficulty in keeping up with his class has yielded the largest percentage of non-returns. This is owing partly to the difficulty in giving a reply under this head in the case of children in the younger classes, and partly to one of the largest schools having misunderstood the question and left it altogether unanswered. This column, however, is one of the least important, and was only inserted in my form to ascertain if possible whether in certain classes any particular subject was regarded as specially difficult, so as to lead to the conclusion that that subject was being too much forced at the stage of education corresponding with these classes.

As it is important for the development of the child that it should go early to bed and get plenty of sleep, especially when much intellectual work is required of it, I have extended my inquiry to this point also. With regard to nourishment, another important factor, I have taken it for granted that children of the class we are dealing with are sufficiently well cared for in this respect; besides, it would have been very difficult to obtain information on this point through the medium of printed forms. I may add, however, that it is expressly stated in many cases that, whereas the children have good appetites during the holidays, they fall off in this respect during the school-term —a statement which many parents and doctors will confirm from their own experience.

By desire of the schools, the forms were sent out in the autumn months, the majority of them in October and the first half of November, while several schools only circulated theirs towards the end of November. The reasons given by the schools for choosing this period was because it is not broken up by any holidays of importance, and because at this season of the year the school work is carried on under the most normal conditions and with least excitement, so that the most truthful results might be expected. This is quite true, but it must also be remembered that the autumn is the most favourable time for the school's side of the case. It is evident that the children are in their best condition for work a couple of months after the summer holidays—the longest period of rest which they enjoy in the year. If the school does exercise a bad effect upon the children's health, such injury will hardly have had time to assert itself prominently so soon after the holidays, so that among school-children, as throughout the community at large, the state of health is at its best in the autumn. It is an old experience of doctors that it is not in the autumn but in the spring, after the long and darksome winter days, that the largest number of cases of anæmia and nervousness, from which so many children, especially young girls, suffer, and of headache, from which boys so frequently suffer, present themselves. These circumstances, to which I attach much importance, must be borne in mind in the following investigation, which, being founded on an inquiry carried on in the autumn, necessarily exhibits the *minimum* of weakly and sickly children.

It is essential I should explain what I mean by sickly children. Many headmasters have tried to prove to me from the school sick-lists that the state of health in their schools is excellent; but the sick-lists are of no value on this point, for they merely show the number of children who are absent owing to temporary illness. It is not to such cases of temporary illness that I refer when I speak of sickly children. By " sickly " I mean *unsound children, who suffer from chronic complaints, but who are, nevertheless, able to attend school regularly; in short, children whose state of health is abnormal, and who require special care, both at home and at school, during their growth and development.* It is only such cases which have been collected here and designated as sickly; properly speaking, they ought to be called cases of *unsound* or *abnormal* health. All children, therefore, who have been returned in the forms as merely suffering from an acute and temporary illness have been included among the healthy. Only when the returns have stated that the child is an habitual sufferer from some definite complaint, or that he is generally delicate, have I put down the case under the heading sickly; in every single case I have carefully considered how to set it down, and if I have erred at all in this matter it has rather been in including sickly children among the healthy than *vice versa*. Cases of "delicate constitution," "worms," "coughs," or other such indefinite ailments, without further statement as to whether the complaint was recurrent or only temporary, as well as cases of "rapid growth," etc., have been put down either as healthy or non-returned, although it is pretty certain that more or less delicate children are to be found in the above categories, especially those suffering from the disease popularly called "worms."

The complaints to which I have ascribed most importance are anæmia, scrofula, nervousness, headache, bleeding at the nose (as a symptom of a tendency to congestion of the brain), curvature of the spine, and diseases of the eye. I had also a column for "other complaints," chief of which are consumption, organic weakness of the heart, chronic affection of the kidneys, epilepsy, St. Vitus's dance, chronic catarrh, weakness resulting from lengthened illnesses, such as diphtheria, rheumatic fever, etc.—diseases which all tend in a great degree to weaken the child's constitution, but for which the school cannot be held directly responsible. Last of all, a column was set apart for "casual complaints," under which heading come cases of rupture and diseases of the joints, both of which prevent children taking part in gymnastics, besides cases of deafness and chronic diseases of the ear, as it has often been stated in the returns that these complaints prevented the children from making equal progress with the others. The above are entirely chronic complaints, which all produce a more or less marked state of weakness in the child.

It will be seen from the above statement that I have far more separate headings than are generally employed in stating cases of ill health among school-

children; for example, in the Swedish statistics. I
have specially desired this, my main object having
been to gather information as to the collective
number of those delicate children who require
special attention on the part of the school, and
stand in need of good hygienic conditions. To
put down headache, anæmia, and nervousness as
specific school complaints would be erroneous, as
the returns show that many children suffer from
them before going to school, although, as may be
supposed, attendance at school often greatly aggra-
vates such complaints.

I am bound to admit one shortcoming in these
returns, namely, that the health column has not as
a rule been filled up by a doctor. I have several
times requested the parents, through the medium
of the school authorities, to let a medical man
fill in this column, but the forms themselves
contained no such direction, as some households
have no family doctor, and I feared that in such
cases no returns at all might be sent in. I cannot
therefore venture to attach much importance to the
special diagnoses of the various complaints, but
consider it, nevertheless, perfectly safe to include

the cases I have done under the category of delicate, sickly children. It is very improbable indeed that any perfectly sound and healthy child should be returned as sickly, and as suffering, moreover, from specified complaints, as we are rather accustomed not to subject the health of a child to too rigid an examination in order to pass it as healthy.

On the other hand, in order to have a complete insight into the physical condition of our school-children we ought to have a thorough examination of their eyesight, but that has not yet been instituted at any school in this country. It will probably be known to many of my readers, however, that in other countries the eyesight of school-children has been a matter of investigation in many instances—with special reference to short-sightedness—and that the results have been anything but satisfactory, especially as far as the classical schools are concerned. The importance of such an examination, though very possibly it may sometimes have been exaggerated, is nevertheless so great, that an inquiry of the kind in our own country is sincerely to be wished for. The few cases of optical complaints given in the returns prove very little; amongst the younger children the optical affection is in the majority of cases probably only a form of scrofula, though amongst the elder ones many cases of short-sightedness are emphatically stated to exist. Even if we take the most favourable returns of optical complaints given in other countries, it would, in the boys' schools at least, double the percentage of unsound children, as will be seen from the following statistics, taken from Dr. Colsman's work, *Die überhandnehmende Kurzsichtigkeit der deutschen Jugend*. The figures give the percentage of short-sighted pupils in each class, the sixth being the youngest.

TABLE I.

	Number examined.	VI.	V.	IV.	III.	II.	I.
Konigsberg .	1518	11	15	20	24	49	62
Hamburg. .	413	14	21	45	40	48	61
Magdeburg I.	650	23	29.	39	63	58	75
Magdeburg II.	776	23	27	42	47	56	70

These figures show to what extent short-sightedness prevails in the German schools, and how it gradually increases from the lower to the higher classes. It is possible that our condition in this respect is better than that of Germany, but a minute examination, official if possible, is absolutely necessary.

CHAPTER II

BOYS' SCHOOLS.

THE information here collected has been taken from fourteen schools, viz. from all the Copenhagen schools which have both the classical and modern sides, and from three of the largest preparatory schools.[1] As the number of classes in each of these sections is fixed by law, and as by private arrangement the number of preparatory or mixed classes[2] is limited to five or six, it has been possible for me to arrange the children by classes throughout, so that a review of the gradual progress at the different ages is obtained.

We shall first consider the general health of

[1] In the original the names of the schools are given, but I have not thought it necessary to reproduce them here. —(TRANS.)

[2] All the classes in the lower section of the school, which is not divided into classical and modern sides, as well as the preparatory classes, are here called "mixed classes."—(TRANS.)

the boys. The comparison between healthy and sickly children will be given in percentages throughout, but we can of course only attach importance to the greatest contrasts; 2 or 3 per cent more or less can hardly be regarded as important, as we must allow some margin for chance inaccuracies.

The fourteen schools have a total of 3141 boys, of whom there were—healthy 1900, sickly 978, while in the case of 263 the returns were insufficient or altogether wanting. The respective percentages are—healthy 60·5, sickly 31·1, non-returned 8·4.

We thus find that out of the total number of boys actually returned one-third is made up of sickly boys, suffering more or less from various chronic complaints. This is truly a sad and startling result, and quite enough to justify the complaints made about the health of our children. The proportion of healthy to sickly children in the different classes is clearly shown on Chart I. The uppermost curve gives the percentage of healthy, the middle one of sickly children, and the lowest that of non-returns. In order to get a criterion of the health of the children on entering school, so as to be able to judge of the influence of school life upon their health, I have taken the two youngest mixed classes together. In many schools there are only five mixed classes, and where there are six the first or youngest may generally be regarded as an infant class, in which formal lessons are but seldom given; these two classes, for all practical purposes, may therefore be taken as one. For these two classes, then, we get the following returns :—healthy 74 per cent, sickly 18·4, non-returned 7·6; which may be taken as a criterion of the health of the children on entering school. That among 369 pupils there should be 18·4 per cent of sickly ones, although the children come from the best homes, shows more clearly than anything else could do how weakly the rising generation has become, how great the tendency to disease is at so early an age, and how watchful we should be with regard to physical development. It follows therefore, as a matter of course, that such an all-powerful factor as school-life, with its demands upon the tender intellect, and the obligation to remain quiet for hours together—not infrequently in a close and unhealthy atmosphere—must exercise a considerable influence upon the health of the child. And indeed we see that in the third mixed class the state of things has become much worse ; the figures are—healthy 56·9, sickly 34·0, non-returned 9·1. *The number of sickly children is almost doubled.* It is difficult to imagine any other important cause for this remarkable increase of unhealthiness than just school life and its demands. With a few unimportant fluctuations the proportions are almost the same throughout the other mixed classes, the proportion in the sixth mixed class being—healthy 58·4, sickly 33·5, non-returned 8·1.

Taking all the mixed classes together the results are—1742 children : healthy 1084, sickly 520, non-returned 138. Percentage: healthy 62·2, sickly 29·9, non-returned 7·9. At the age of about twelve the pupil passes from the mixed classes into either the classical or modern division, each of which must be considered separately.

Modern Division.—In the first modern class a marked increase in the percentage of sickly children is observed, that class giving a larger percentage than any other modern class, viz.—healthy 49·7, sickly 38·8, non-returned 11·5. In the second class the proportion of healthy pupils rises to 59·7 per cent, and remains thereabouts in the higher classes. The percentage of sickly falls at the same time in the next three classes to 30·9 in the second, 24·3 in the third, and 23·4 in the fourth, but this is partly owing to the exceptional number of non-returns (*vide* the curve on Chart I.) In the fourth modern class we get—healthy 57·8, sickly 23·4, non-returned 18·8, while the total for the modern classes is—healthy 300, sickly 165, non-returned 66. Percentage : healthy 56·5, sickly 31·1, non-returned 12·4.

Classical Division.—In the first classical class the relations are the same as in the sixth mixed class, but in the second classical class a rise in the percentage of sickly pupils takes place similar to that which was observed in the first modern class, the percentages now standing—healthy 50·5, sickly 41·9, non-returned 7·6 ; which is the highest per-centage of sickly children found in any class. In the third classical class the percentage of sickly boys drops suddenly to 31·8, while those of the

healthy and non-returned are 63·0 and 5·2 respectively. The fourth class is about the same, but in the
fifth class the figures are—healthy 60·5, sickly 38·2,
non-returned 1·3 ; changing to healthy 60·4, sickly
26·4, non-returned 13·2 in the sixth class. These
apparently great variations in the fifth and sixth
classes are, however, accounted for by the number
of non-returns, viz. 1·3 in the fifth and 13·2 in
the sixth class, which powerfully affects the percentage of the sickly, while that of the healthy remains
pretty stationary in the four highest classes (*vide* the
Tables), ranging only from 63·0 to 60·4. For the
rhetorical section of the classical school we get the
following results :—783 pupils: healthy 458, sickly
269, non-returned 56. Percentage : healthy 58·5,
sickly 34·4, non-returned 7·1; which is rather
more unfavourable than in the modern classes.

In the mathematical and natural science section there is only a total of 85 pupils, of whom
there are—healthy 58, sickly 24, non-returned 3.
Percentage: healthy 68·2, sickly 28·3, non-returned
3·5. If we take the two highest classical forms
(both the rhetorical and mathematical) and regard
the figures thus obtained as giving a criterion of

the state of health on leaving school, we get out of 169 pupils—healthy 107, sickly 53, non-returned 9. Percentage: healthy 63·3, sickly 31·1, non-returned 5·3, *i.e. exactly one-third of the pupils being sickly ;* while we must also bear in mind that no special examination of their eyesight has taken place, the importance of which I have already mentioned.

Specially worthy of note is the sudden rise in the percentage of sickly boys in the first modern and second classical forms, and the equally sudden fall in this percentage immediately afterwards. It is manifestly the same cause that is at work in inducing this rapid development of sickliness in both cases, while the fact of the rise and subsequent fall taking place earlier in the modern class than in the classical may probably be accounted for by the slight difference between the average age of this class and that of the corresponding classical one, viz. 12·8 years in the first modern and 12·5 years in the first classical. The common cause of the increased sickliness in both instances is evidently to be found in the development into manhood, which commences about the thirteenth year, and during which the whole organism of the boy undergoes a complete change. It would now appear that this change is preceded by a short period of greater delicacy than usual, with greater susceptibility to unfavourable external influences. How radical is the change which at this time takes place in the constitution of the child is clearly shown by the following statement as to growth and weight for those particular years during which it is going on. As the result of a series of very carefully-conducted investigations, Dr. Kotelmann, in his treatise on *Die Körperverhältnisse der Gelehrtenschüler des Johanneum in Hamburg*,[1] gives the following figures:—

TABLE II.

Ages.	Increase in Height.	Increase in Weight.
9-12	5·71 inches.	19 lbs.
13-16	9·37 ,,	44 ,,
17-20	2·43 ,,	23 ,,

From the seventeenth to the twentieth year the increase, particularly in height, is but slight. The figures for each year separately show that it

---

[1] "The physical characteristics of the pupils of the Johanneum in Hamburg."

is just at the age of thirteen that development goes on most rapidly. It is exactly the same with regard to the development of the muscular tissue, and of the chest, and indeed of the whole body,—growth goes on at a rapid rate during the years of puberty, from thirteen to sixteen, and much more slowly after that period. The importance of that stage of a boy's life has always been recognised, but the few figures quoted above show the exceeding importance of allowing free scope to the boy's development at that epoch. This development, both in body and mind, is one of nature's processes, and if it be forced or retarded in one direction or the other the boy is sure to suffer, and the consequences may never be completely got over.

If we now review the facts we have collected we find that a considerable proportion of children —18 per cent, or about one-fifth—are sickly or weakly on entering school. This shows that the children on coming from their homes are affected by ill health, or have a tendency towards it in considerable proportion. But the facts that the percentage of sickly children, after a couple of

years, advances to 30 per cent, and suddenly rises
to 40 per cent shortly before puberty, indicate how
great is the influence which school experiences,
alone or in conjunction with developmental processes, undoubtedly exercise upon the health of
boys. Even when the body recovers itself after
its supreme effort of growth, as it does in the following years, the percentage of sickly children is only
reduced to about 30 per cent, at which it remains
throughout the highest classes. No comparison
with children who do not go to school, or rather
who receive no school education, can of course
take place in a country where school attendance
is obligatory on all children; but I do not believe
that any other important factor can be pointed to
which exercises an influence upon the child's life,
between the ages of eight and twelve, at all ade-
quate to explain the deterioration of health which
has been referred to, besides school life, and the
entire change in the habits and feelings of the child
which it involves. The discipline of school, with
its strictly-defined hours of sedentary work, is in
itself no slight contrast to that prior state of existence in which the boy's natural propensity to romp

and play was allowed free scope. It must therefore, I think, be regarded as an established fact,
that school as now conducted, with all the con-
comitants of school life, undoubtedly exercises a
pernicious influence upon the health of the child.
This pernicious influence cannot perhaps be altogether avoided, but it certainly ought not to be so
powerful for evil as it is here shown to be. I
am far from asserting that school life is the sole
cause of the prevalent sickliness among schoolboys,
but it is certain that it plays the principal part
in its production, and that its influence can be
more clearly proved than any other.

Whereas the proportion of sickly children is
31 per cent for the total number of schools, it
naturally varies in the case of individual schools.
It ranges between 25 per cent, which is the lowest
figure any school can produce, and 35 per cent;
only in a single instance, to which I shall again
have occasion to refer, does the percentage come
up to 39.

TABLE III.

Class	HEALTHY	Anæmia	Scrofula	Nervousness	Headache	Bleeding at the Nose	Curvature of the Spine	Diseases of the Eye	Other Complaints	Casual Complaints	TOTAL	NON-RETURNED	Healthy (%)	Sickly (%)	Non-Returns (%)
1st Mixed	117	3	14	5	..	1	1	1	4	3	30	14	72·7	18·6	8·7
2d do.	156	7	17	8	5	3	..	1	3	1	38	14	75·0	18·3	6·7
3d do.	169	13	21	31	22	7	2	3	18	8	101	27	56·9	30·4	9·1
4th do.	226	17	38	27	23	10	..	5	10	9	111	24	62·6	30·7	6·7
5th do.	214	19	40	25	38	9	1	4	14	6	124	31	58·0	33·6	8·4
6th do.	202	17	21	28	32	12	5	5	17	3	116	28	58·4	33·5	8·1
TOTAL	1084	76	151	124	120	42	9	19	66	30	520	138	62·2	29·9	7·9
PERCENTAGE	...	12	24	19	19	7	1	3	10	5	...	...	...	...	...
1st Mrn	82	11	5	15	26	4	2	2	7	6	64	19	49·7	38·8	11·5
2d do.	114	9	10	12	24	4	1	5	6	4	59	18	59·7	30·9	9·4
3d do.	67	4	4	6	12	4	..	1	5	2	27	17	60·4	24·3	15·3
4th do.	37	...	3	2	7	2	..	2	4	1	15	12	57·8	23·4	18·8
TOTAL	300	24	22	35	69	14	3	10	22	13	165	66	56·5	31·1	12·4
PERCENTAGE	...	11	10	17	32	7	2	5	10	6	...	...	...	...	...

	C1	C2	C3	C4	C5	C6	C7	C8	C9	C10	C11	C12	C13	C14	C15
1st Classical	142	16	16	25	19	7	2	1	9	2	79	20	58·9	32·8	8·3
2d do.	94	11	19	18	24	6	2	3	8	3	78	14	50·5	41·9	7·6
3d do.	85	7	3	6	17	4	...	4	6	4	43	7	63·0	31·8	5·2
4th do.	59	7	2	1	12	2	...	3	4	3	26	7	64·1	28·3	7·6
5th do.	46	3	2	7	6	7	...	6	2	5	29	1	60·5	38·2	1·3
6th do.	32	...	1	3	5	1	...	4	1	...	14	7	60·4	26·4	13·2
TOTAL (Rhetorical Section)	458	44	43	60	83	27	4	21	30	17	269	56	58·5	34·4	7·1
PERCENTAGE	...	14	13	18	25	8	1	7	9	5	...	...	...	...	...
3d Classical / 6th do. (Natural Science Section)	58	4	2	5	12	3	1	3	...	4	24	3	68·2	28·3	3·5
PERCENTAGE	...	12	5	15	35	9	3	9	...	12	...	...	...	...	...
TOTAL for Boys' Schools	1900	148	218	224	284	86	17	53	118	64	978	263	60·5	31·1	8·4
PERCENTAGE	...	12	18	19	24	7	1	4	10	5	...	...	...	...	...
1st & 2d Mixed	273	10	31	13	5	4	1	2	7	4	68	28	74·0	18·4	7·6
PERCENTAGE	...	13	42	17	6	5	1	2	9	5	...	...	...	...	...
5th & 6th Classical (Rhetorical and Natural Science Sections)	107	4	3	13	16	10	...	11	3	6	53	9	63·3	31·4	5·3
PERCENTAGES	...	6	5	19	24	15	...	17	5	9	...	...	...	...	...

Particulars as to the different complaints to which schoolboys are liable are given in Table III., and with regard to these I shall confine myself to a few remarks. Scrofula, it will be observed, occupies the foremost place among the complaints of boys up to fourteen,—the age of puberty,—after which only a small percentage of boys suffer from that disease; this holds good for girls as well as boys, and corresponds with results derived from other sources. I would specially direct attention to the distinctive nature of the complaints respectively prevalent in the youngest and oldest classes. In the two youngest classes scrofula is recorded as the most common complaint, whereas, when we get to the two highest classes, we find that the cases of headache and bleeding at the nose—both indications of a tendency to congestion of the brain—and diseases of the eye have greatly increased. This would appear to be a strong proof that the mental work plays a momentous part in the deterioration of health in schoolboys. That the number of cases enumerated exceeds the total number of sickly children is of course explained by the fact that a child may have more than one complaint at the same time. Thus, for example, of the eighty-six boys subject to bleedings at the nose, thirty-eight were stated to be suffering at the same time from other complaints, and in particular from headaches.

A comparison of Danish schools with those of other countries would be very interesting; but schools in other countries are in many respects so differently constituted from ours, and such information as has been collected in them is arranged so differently from mine, that no detailed comparison is possible. I shall therefore merely allude briefly to some points of interest in connection with Swedish, German, and Norwegian schools. To each of the classical schools in Sweden a medical officer is appointed, whose duty it is twice a year to report systematically upon the health of the seminary under his charge. This regulation, which has only just come into force, was last year carried into effect in the case of a few schools. I append the results obtained from two of them, viz. the New Elementary School in Stockholm and the Landskrona General Institute.

TABLE IV.

	Number of Pupils.	Age.	Physique.			General State of Health.		Anæmia.	Headache.	Bleeding at Nose.	Short-sightedness.
			Good.	Middling.	Weak.	Good.	Not Good.				
New Elementary School . . .	299	11-18	218	41	40	241	58	38	38	19	105
PERCENTAGE.	...	...	73	14	13	80	20	13	13	6	35
Landskrona General Institute .	119	10-14	12	83	24	...	...	31	14	8	11
PERCENTAGE.	...	...	10	70	20	...	...	26	12	7	9

The above table does not show whether the number of cases of complaints represent an equal number of sickly children, or whether some of the children, for example, have had headache in conjunction with bleeding at the nose. My schedules, too, contain a greater number of different headings than does this one, as, for example, scrofula (cases of nervousness, probably, being generally included under anæmia), so that a complete comparison is impossible. There is also a striking difference between the two schools included in this table, especially as regards the physique of the children

attending them, so that the collection and treatment of the materials in the two can hardly have
been the same.

The Hours of Work in the Different Classes.

The daily work of school children consists
partly of the regular school work and partly of
preparation and written exercises done at home,
to which, in many cases, private tuition in one or
more subjects has to be added; but it is of course
to the work demanded by the school that the
greatest importance attaches. Table V. and Chart
II. show the number of hours of work of the pupils
in each class. The intervals for play—generally
a quarter of an hour at a time—are included
throughout in the hours of work, as is the case
with the German, Norwegian, and Swedish statistics, singing and gymnastics being also thus
included. We thus see that the daily school
work—*i.e.* the number of hours spent at school
and in preparation at home—is 4·6 hours in
the first mixed class, after which it rises rapidly
in the following classes until we get 7·7 hours in

CLASS.	Number of Pupils.	Ages.	Average Age.	WEEKLY.							
				Number of Hours at School.	Languages.	Written Exercises.	Singing.	Drawing.	Writing.	Gymnastics.	Total.
1st Mixed	161	5– 9	6·6	24	...	...	0–1	...	0–10	0–5	3–1
2d do.	208	5– 9	7·5	24–30	...	0–3	0–1	0–1	2–8	0–6	3–1
3d do.	297	6–10	8·5	22–33	0– 6	0–4	0–2	0–2	–6	2–	7
4th do.	361	7–13	9·6	28–33	3– 6	0–5	0–2	0–2	–6	2–	6–
5th do.	369	8–13	10·5	28–36	6– 9	0–4	0–2	0–2	–6	2–	5–
6th do.	346	9–14	11·7	30–36	6–11	0–4	0–2	0–2	–7	–	6
Total	1742										
1st Modern	165	10–15	12·8	32–36	9–11	2–6	0–2	1–2	1–3	2–4	5–1
2d do.	191	11–16	13·8	31–36	9–11	1·5–7	0–2	0–2	1–3	2–5	4–1
3d do.	111	12–16	14·6	31–36	6–15	1·5–8	0–2	0–3	0–2	0–3	3–
4th do.	64	14–17	15·6	32–36	9–15	2·5–6	0–1	0–2	0–1	0–3	0–
Total	531										
1st Classical	241	10–15	12·5	33–36	11–14	2–7	0–2	0–2	1–2	2–4	4–
2d do.	186	11–15	13·5	33–36	11–16	1·8–6	0–2	0–1	0–2	2–4	3–
3d do.	135	13–16	14·5	33–36	11–19	2·5–8	0–2	...	0–1	2–4	2–
4th do.	92	13–18	15·4	34–36	16–19	1·5–7·5	0–2	...	...	2–4	2–
5th do.	76	14–21	16·6	32–36	20–22	1·8–3·5	0–2	...	...	2–4	2–
6th do.	53	16–21	17·5	33–38	19–24	2–4·5	0–1	...	...	0–4	0–
Total	783										
3d Nat. Science	30	12–16	14·1	33–36	11–13	2·5–4·5	0–2	1–2	0–1	2–4	3–
4th do.	15	14–17	15·7	34–36	12–14	2·5–4	0–2	1–2	...	2–4	3–
5th do.	23	15–18	16·9	30–36	7– 8	4–11	0–2	0–3	...	1–4	1–
6th do.	17	16–19	17·5	27–35	7– 8	3·5–9	...	0–3	...	0–4	0–
Total	85										
TOTAL	3141										

Hours occupied in Work at Home.	Hours occupied in Work at School.	School + Extra Work.	School Work according to place in Class.			Private Tuition Weekly.					Dancing.	Gymnastics.
			1	2	3	Number of Pupils.	Percentage.	Music.	Languages.	Other Subjects.		
)·6	4·6	5·1	4·6	4·5	5·5	2	1·2	2	...	...	16	...
·1	5·4	6·2	5·4	5·4	5·7	17	8·2	13	1	3	40	6
·4	6·2	7·1	6·0	6·2	6·4	57	19·2	47	1	9	87	5
·8	6·9	7·8	6·6	7·0	7·2	73	20·0	60	2	11	92	5
2·0	7·4	8·1	7·1	7·5	7·8	124	33·6	102	3	19	91	15
2·0	7·7	8·5	7·3	7·8	7·7	101	29·2	89	3	9	98	11
						374	21·5	313	10	51	424	42
·3	8·0	8·9	7·5	8·2	7·9	60	35·8	43	7	10	24	12
·7	8·5	9·4	8·8	9·4	8·8	69	30·9	40	9	20	32	7
·8	8·5	9·1		·		38	34·2	23	2	13	11	3
·4	9·0	9·3		·		29	45·3	17	2	10	1	2
						196	36·7	123	20	53	68	24
·4	8·2	9·0	8·0	8·3	8·4	98	40·7	75	4	19	43	4
·7	8·4	9·5	8·3	8·6	8·3	78	41·9	70	3	5	48	7
·3	9·1	9·7	9·2	9·1	9·2	54	40·0	41	2	11	22	5
·6	9·4	10·0	9·1	9·7	9·5	37	40·2	24	6	7	5	1
·3	10·0	11·1	9·6	10·2	9·8	24	31·6	15	6	3	2	1
·5	10·4	11·2	9·7	10·6	10·7	13	24·5	11	2	...	1	...
						304	38·8	236	23	45	121	18
·2	8·9	9·5	8·8	8·6	9·5	12	40·0	7	3	2	2	...
·4	·3	0·5	9·2	9·2	9·8	10	66·6	4	3	3	3	1
·8	·4	1·2			·7	6	26·1	3	3	...	1	1
·1	·6	·9			1·2	6	35·3	5	...	1	1	...
						34	40·0	19	9	6	8	2
				TOTAL		908	28·7	691	62	155	621	86
		PERCENTAGE OF PUPILS			· ·			22·0	2·0	4·7	20·0	2·4
		Do.	OF EXTRA WORK					76·1	6·8	17·1		

the sixth mixed class, being an average increase of half an hour per class. In the preparatory schools the hours are a little longer in the two highest classes, amounting in the sixth class to eight hours *per diem*, but this is naturally accounted for by the fact that the children are about to be sent to more advanced schools, for places in which there is lively competition, so that they have to be brought on further than would otherwise be the case.

The work hours go on increasing in the higher classes, but somewhat irregularly. In the modern section they only increase from eight hours in the first to nine hours in the fourth and highest class, being the smallest advance among the higher classes. The greatest increase in the work hours takes place in the classical side of the different schools, especially in the rhetorical section, viz. from 8·2 hours in the first classical to 10·4 in the sixth class, the greatest rise being from 8·4 in the second to 9·1 in the third class, almost three-quarters of an hour. In the natural science section 9·6 hours in the highest class is the longest day's work, but the small number of pupils in this section tends to make the result more uncertain.

The work demanded by the school in the four highest classical classes is thus very considerable, occupying nearly ten and a half hours daily.

As already stated, 908 pupils, or 28·7 per cent of the whole number, have private tuition over and above the work done in and for the school, and this increases the daily work by about three-quarters of an hour, though, as shown in Table V., the additional burden thus entailed varies some-what in amount in the different classes. This is no inconsiderable addition to the ordinary work, and in the case of pupils in the highest classes, whose time is already so much taken up, the effect of this extra labour must be very appreciable. It brings up their daily average of work to eleven hours.

The Distribution of Subjects in the Different Classes.

Table V. gives the number of hours spent at school, and an analysis of the hours devoted to several subjects, as, for example, languages and those other subjects which do not demand so much mental effort. A considerable difference is observable between the various schools, and I endeavoured to calculate the averages, but as these proved rather uncertain and hardly in accordance with the true state of things I did not insert them. The considerable fluctuations with regard to the written exercises are partly attributable to the different ways in which the mathematical exercises have been regarded in answering that question.

Can the daily work here shown to be required in Danish schools be said to be excessive? This brings us face to face with the extremely difficult question as to how much work a boy can undertake without detriment at a particular age, and the answers given to this question vary considerably. This very question has been the subjcet of an animated discussion in Germany of late years. In 1875 M. Falck, then Minister for Education in Prussia, required information from the schools as to the time employed by the pupils in home preparation. As the outcome of this investigation the *Provinzial Schulcollegium der Provinz Wesphalen* issued a circular, dated 5th January 1876, in which, after referring to the great diversities in the returns from the different schools, it is stated : "On account of this want of uniformity in the results we beg to refer to the unanimous resolution at the fifteenth conference of Westphalian School Directors, by which the time to be spent in home preparation by pupils of ordinary capacity was limited to a maximum of four hours daily for the upper, three for the middle, and two for the lower classes, including all private reading which the pupil had to do." This circular was inserted in the ministerial paper and thus officially recognised as valid for Prussia, and in order to appreciate its full significance we want to know now how many hours a day are spent at school in that country ; and I therefore append the averages taken from twelve Prussian gymnasia or high schools.[1]

When comparing these Prussian schools with our own it must be borne in mind that the period of school tuition in Prussia is longer than with us, the average age of pupils on leaving these gymnasia being 19·7 years, as compared with 18·1 in Danish schools, so that German boys are a year

[1] I am indebted for the following particulars to the courtesy of M. C. Werner of Halle.

and a half older on leaving school than Danish ones are. In Germany two years are spent in each of the three highest classes, and one year in each of the three lowest, the whole course thus occupying nine years. The average age on leaving school and the daily hours of work in each class in the Prussian gymnasia are as follows :—

TABLE VI.

CLASS.		Age.	Weekly Total of School Hours.	Gymnastics and Singing.	Home Work daily.	Number of Hours of daily Work.
VI.		11½	28	3	2	7·2
V.		12½	30	3	2	7·5
IV.		13½	30	3	3	8·5
III.	Lower . . .	14½	30	3	3	8·5
	Upper . . .	15½				
II.	Lower . . .	16½	30	2	4	9·3
	Upper . . .	17½				
I.	Lower . . .	18½	30	2	4	9·3
	Upper . . .	19½				

Thus in the highest classes 9·3 hours' daily work, including singing and gymnastics, is regarded as the extreme limit of permissible application to study. Whether the German pupils really do not exceed that limit I cannot tell, but that is the maximum of daily work, including private tuition, which the instructors of the German youth consider compatible with a due regard for health, and even these regulations as to the hours of work are still deemed too high by pedagogues as well as German doctors.

If we wish to compare the German hours with our own we must do so by age, because, as I have pointed out, the German average in the highest class is a year and a half above our own. It would also appear that we devote more time to gymnastics than the Germans, Copenhagen school-boys having on an average from two to three hours of gymnastics weekly—some of them even four hours—in almost all the classes, while gymnastics only occupy one to two hours weekly in the first and second classes in German schools. Taking my standard mainly from the above expression of opinion by German school authorities, I drew up a scale of "normal" work hours applicable to each class, and then computed how many pupils had "normal" work and how many had more than normal, i.e. "hard work" in Danish schools. Only those cases in which the limit of "normal work" has been exceeded have I included under the heading "hard work." As the hours of work increased gradually from class to class I made out my scale accordingly, and not by such sudden transitions as the German pedagogues allowed. My scale is higher throughout than the German limits, not because I think them too narrow—quite the reverse—but partly because it was not apparent from the German statistics, which I originally used, which subjects were obligatory, so that I took the weekly hours of school work to be longer than I now find they are, and partly because of my desire to escape the accusation of having fixed the limit too low. It is evident that a maximum of 9·3 hours for the highest classes (instead of the ten hours I have taken as my standard of normal work) would show a result even more unfavourable to our schools than the one I shall presently give. Then, again, 9·3 hours is the *maximum*, which is not to be exceeded, so that a fair medium ought rather to be something like nine hours.[1]

The following table shows for each separate class the hours actually spent in work by the pupils, the standard of normal work I have taken,

[1] To prevent all possible misunderstanding let me here express as my personal conviction that what I have taken as the "normal" standard of work is decidedly pitched much too high.

and the maximum decreed by the Germans. The pupils in the corresponding German classes are, moreover, six months older on an average than in ours.

TABLE VII.

CLASS.	Age.	No. of Hours of daily School Work.	No. of Hours of School Work and Private Tuition.	Normal Work	German Maximum.
1st Mixed	7	4·6	5·1	6·0	...
2d do.	8	5·4	6·2	7·3	...
3rd do.	9	6·2	7·1	7·5	...
4th do.	10	6·9	7·8	7·8	...
5th do. (VI.) .	11	7·4	8·1	8·0	7·2
6th do. (V.) .	12	7·7	8·5	8·3	7·5
1st Classical (IV.) .	13	8·2 (8·0)	9·0 (8·9)	8·5	8·5
2d do. (III.) .	14	8·4 (8·5)	9·5 (9·4)	8·8	8·5
3rd do. (III.) .	15	9·1 (8·5)	9·7 (9·1)	9·0	8·5
4th do. (II.) .	16	9·4 (9·0)	10·0 (9.3)	9·0	9·3
5th do. (II.) .	17	10·0	11·1	10·0	9·3
6th do. (I.) .	18	10·4	11·2	10·0	9·3

Particulars as to the hours of work in all the classes will be found in Table V. The ages given for both Danish and German schools are the average ones attained by the pupils at the end of the school year. The figures in brackets in Table VII. show the work hours in the modern classes, the Roman figures indicating the German classes corresponding with those in the Danish schools, the numbers of which they stand opposite.

E

Thus we see that in all the classes, with the exception of the first and second classical, the work hours in the Copenhagen schools exceed the maximum which is considered by the German pedagogues to be permissible. In the case of those pupils who receive private tuition the excess is still greater, and surpasses even the higher standard employed by me.

In the Swedish schools the daily hours of school work appear almost to correspond with our own. Twice a year the Swedish scholars send in a statement of the time employed in preparation and written exercises at home, and I have taken as illustrative the returns for three schools, viz. the New Elementary School in Stockholm, the Caroline Cathedral School in Lund, and the General Educational Institute in Malmö. According to the regular system each class in the classical section has the following number of school hours (including half an hour of gymnastics daily, which is probably the shortest time ever devoted to gymnastics in Swedish schools).

TABLE VIII.

		CLASS.								
		I.	II.	III.	IV.	V.	VI.$_1$	VI.$_2$	VII.$_1$	VII.$_2$
Number of Hours at School . .		5·0	5·5	5·5	5·5	5·5	5·8	5·8	5·5	5.5
Home preparation and written exercises.	Stockholm	1·5	1·5	2·5 to 3·5	3·7	5·4	4·8	...	5·3	...
	Lund . .	1·0	1·5 to 2·0	1·5 to 2·0	2·5	3·5	3·0	5·0	5·0	5·0
	Malmö .	0·5 to 1·0	1·0 to 1·5	1·5 to 2·0	2·0	2·5	3-4	3.4	2·5 to 4·5	5-6

One or two other schools show even higher returns of work done at home, viz.—Kalmar, Class VI.$_1$, six hours; Class VI.$_2$, six to seven hours; Halmsted in 1876, Class VII.$_2$, seven hours ; but these are exceptional cases.

It seems that the home work done by Swedish schoolboys is rather heavier than in our country (where the longest time spent in preparation is 4·5 hours daily), at least amongst the higher classes. When reviewing the work done in Swedish schools, however, we must remember that the holidays, and especially the summer vacations, are much longer in them than with us, and that the average age, on leaving school, is nineteen years as against eighteen in Denmark. The school time is divided into forenoon and afternoon sessions, not more than two or at the outside three hours of continuous work being allowed, after which an interval of at least two hours is compulsory. With us the school hours are not broken up by longer intervals than a quarter of an hour at a time, and schools are even known to exist in which, after five hours of school work, without any break whatever, the pupils have to spend other two hours in preparation, making seven continuous hours of brain labour. One long uninterrupted spell of work such as this is much more exhausting to children than a like duration of work broken up into portions of two or three hours each, with as many intervals.

In Norway the question of children's school work has been subjected to a very minute investigation. In 1865 a Royal Commission was appointed to consider a revision of the education code for advanced schools. The schools were required by the Commission to furnish statistics as to the school work, and the results (which are to be found in the seventh and eighth volumes of the Norwegian School and University Annals) are very interesting in many respects. Several schools, through their official spokesmen, state that their pupils are overloaded with work; and all of them protest vigorously against any increase in the demands made for the Examination in Arts which is taken on leaving school.

From Stavanger school the statement comes that many pupils in the highest classes work eleven hours daily.

Herr Vibe, rector in Christiania, reports that the school work is five and six hours daily, and the home work as follows:—

TABLE IX.

1st Class . . .	1 Hour	54	Minutes.
2d ,, . . .	2 Hours	19	,,
3d ,, . . .	2 ,,	29	,,
4th ,, . . .	3 ,,	39	,,
5th ,, . . .	3 ,,	56	,,
6th ,, . . .	3 ,,	14	,,
7th ,, . . .	2 ,,	30	,,

He declares this to be "much too much," and speaks of the present state of things as "an over-loading with educational matter, and consequent apathy and want of interest on the part of the pupil, an overtaxing of youthful strength, a con-stant driving and forcing on in every subject"

(vol. viii. p. 269).   The college of teachers of
Tromsö school declare eight hours of sedentary
work, exclusive of gymnastics, to be the maximum
of permissible school teaching.   Several teachers
point out besides that although the school hours
may not be longer than they formerly were, yet,
the subject-matter now demanded being much
more difficult and requiring more concentrated
attention on the part of the learners than was the
case thirty years ago, the work is altogether much
more exhausting.

In its Report the Norwegian School Commission
(part i. p. 214) expresses its opinion that the work
prescribed for the Arts Examination should and
could be less exacting in many subjects than it
now is, though the Commission does not regard the
heavy demands of this examination as chiefly to
blame for the grievous overpressure which exists
in many schools ; it attributes this rather to an im-
proper method of teaching, for which the teachers
are mainly responsible, as well as to the use of
bad school books, etc.   The principal reason
given by the Commission for not considering the
demands excessive is that in the Danish schools

the prescribed work is much greater, and that a Commission of Danish pedagogues had declared that no danger of overpressure could possibly arise in their highly favoured land. Thus at page 109 of the Report it is stated—"In these (the Danish) schools the pupils have to get up more Latin and Greek than is prescribed by our code. Besides this, Natural History, Physics, and Astronomy are taught from advanced books, as well as Conic Sections, Plain and Spherical Trigonometry. In our Norwegian schools the subjects taken instead of all these are only Church History and, as a voluntary subject, English." That the authorities attached considerable importance to the "much greater" demands instituted by the Danish code is also apparent from a circular, dated 6th February 1867, issued to the schools by the Education Department, in which this point is specially emphasised.

At the instigation of school teachers the Medical Society of Christiania made the question of overpressure the subject of a discussion, which extended throughout seven sittings (vide *Norwegian Magazine of Medical Science*, 1866-67). A large

number of the most eminent physicians took part
in the discussion, and all without exception
declared it to be decidedly their experience that
school children—boys as well as girls—were as a
rule overburdened with work, greatly to the pre-
judice of their bodily and mental development.
It was significantly pointed out at the time that
there had seldom been unanimity so striking on
any subject on the part of the medical profession.
Now it is to be remembered that the Danish school
code was stated to be much more exacting, as to
its demands for the Arts Examination, than the
Norwegian one.

Having thus briefly glanced at one or two
features of the educational systems in neighbouring
countries, I will proceed to give the result obtained by applying my standard of "normal" work
to the schools more immediately under discussion.

Table X. shows the number of pupils in each
class who have "normal" and "super-normal"
work, showing, at the same time, in what proportion any excess of work beyond the normal limit
is due to school work alone or to private study.

Seventy-two per cent, *i.e.* almost three-fourths

TABLE X.

CLASS.	NORMAL STANDARD. No. of Hours.	NORMAL WORK. No. of Pupils.	Percentage.	HARD WORK. No. of Pupils.	Percentage.	School Work.	Extra Work.	NON-RETURNED. No. of Pupils.	Percentage.
1st Mixed . .	6·0	153	95·0	2	1·2	2	...	6	3·8
2d do. . .	7·3	201	96·2	2	1·0	1	1	6	2·8
3d do. . .	7·5	270	91·2	19	6·4	13	6	7	2·4
4th do. . .	7·8	286	79·2	67	18·6	45	22	8	2·2
5th do. . .	8·0	261	70·7	105	28·5	64	41	3	0·8
6th do. . .	8·3	235	67·9	108	31·2	77	31	3	0·9
		1406	80·7	303	17·4	202	101	33	1·9
						67%	33%		
1st Modern . .	8·5	114	69·1	51	30·9	37	14	...	...
2d do. . .	8·8	111	58·1	80	41·9	59	21	...	...
3d do. . .	9·0	77	69·4	34	30·6	21	13	...	...
4th do. . .	9·0	32	50·0	32	50·0	26	6	...	...
		334	62·9	197	37·1	143	54	...	...
						73%	27%		
1st Classical (*Rhet.*)	8·5	145	60·2	95	39·4	66	29	1	0·4
2d do.	8·8	95	51·1	85	45·7	60	25	6	3·2
3d do.	9·0	51	37·8	82	60·7	55	27	2	1·5
4th do.	9·0	28	30·4	64	69·6	57	7	...	...
5th do.	10·0	41	54·7	35	45·3	31	4	...	...
6th do.	10·0	22	41·5	31	58·5	30	1	...	...
		382	48·8	392	50·2	299	93	9	1·0
						76%	24%		
3d Classical (*Natural Science*)	9·0	13	43·3	17	56·7	12	5	...	...
4th do.	9·0	4	26·6	11	73·4	9	2	...	...
5th do.	10·0	14	60·9	7	30·4	4	3	2	8·7
6th do.	10·0	12	70·6	5	29·4	3	2	...	...
		43	50·6	40	47·1	28	12	2	2·3
						70%	30%		
TOTAL		2165	68·9	932	29·7	672	260	44	1·4
						72%	28%		

of the total number of cases of hard work, are due
to school studies alone, leaving only 28 per cent
due to private study.   The pressure of the school
work is seen to be most severe from the fourth to
the sixth classical rhetorical section.   Thus about
one-third of the total number of pupils have hard
work; while in the rhetorical section of the classical side the number of boys who do "hard" work
is greater than the number doing "normal" work,
particularly in the third and fourth classes, where
60 to 70 per cent have hard work.   These are
just the classes, too, in which most overpressure
has always been alleged to exist.   In the fourth
modern class the proportions of normal and of
hard workers are equal.

Now if the German standard had been taken,
the percentage of hard-worked pupils would
have been much greater; for example, in both
sections of the classical side (for which the
maximum is 9·3 hours, including private study)
only 34 pupils out of 169, or 20 per cent,
would have appeared as doing normal work;
whereas 133 pupils, or 79 per cent, would have
been classified as hard-worked, with two cases

(1 per cent) non-returned. According to my standard, however, 89 pupils (53 per cent) of these four classes have normal and 78 (46 per cent) hard work. The difference is seen to be very considerable. Expressed in percentages, the results for each section are as follows :—

TABLE XI.

CLASSES.	Normal Work.	Hard Work.	Non-re-turned.
Mixed	80·7	17·4	1·9
Modern	62·9	37·1	...
Classical (*Rhetorical*) .	48·8	50·2	1·0
Classical (*Natural Science*)	50·6	47·1	2·3
AVERAGE .	68·9	29·7	1·4

The question as to whether the boys in our Copenhagen schools are overworked is now more easily answered. So high a limit of "normal" work has been adopted here that I am sure every one will admit that anything beyond it is really hard work. Besides, this normal standard—which, in the case of most of the classes, is higher than the foreign pedagogues consider right and proper—is only justifiable on the distinct supposition that the pupils are perfectly strong and sound boys. But this is far indeed from being the case, at least one-third, as we have seen, being sickly delicate children, whose state of health demands special consideration, and that, too, just at the age of their school life when the work is most severe, viz. during the period of puberty. I maintain, therefore, most emphatically that the school does not work with strong and healthy children; the proportion of delicate ones among them is so great that it must be taken into special consideration in connection with the demands made upon the pupils in general. The work now demanded of the scholars exceeds, in a very large number of cases, those limits which, even for perfectly sound children, can be admitted to be justifiable. There can therefore be no doubt that the demands made at present upon all groups of schoolboys, but more especially upon those in the classical divisions of schools, and which are fixed by law, are so considerable that the work entailed upon the pupils, in order to fulfil them, must necessarily exercise an injurious influence upon the health of a considerable proportion.

In judging of the ages of our schoolboys in relation to their work, it must also be remembered that the estimated age of, for example, 18 in the sixth class is only attained on leaving school. In the month of November the average age of the boys in that class was 17·5, and those of the boys in other classes in proportion. As the age given for each pupil is the number of years actually completed, they are of course all above the age stated. I have therefore added half a year throughout to the average obtained from the ages returned— that of the sixth class was really 16·9—and I think I have thus got as near to the truth as is possible.

It has often been said that the clever boys in particular have to work hardest. In order to see if this is really the case I requested the schools to state on each schedule whether the pupil to which it referred was reckoned among the cleverest in his class, among those of ordinary ability, or among the dullest. The result is exhibited in Table V., where, under the heading "School Work according to place in Class," 1 marks the cleverest, 2 the ordinary, and 3 the dullest pupils. There does not appear to be any great difference, nor any invariable relation in this respect.

Of the subjects included in the extra or private work music is the most important. Out of the total of 908 boys who have private tuition, 691, or 76·1 per cent, take music lessons, while only 62, or 6·8 per cent, receive private tuition in languages, and 155, or 17·1 per cent, in other subjects, chief of which are mathematics and religious instruction. The numbers for each class are given in Table V. It is principally the pupils in the middle classes who have private study. The work of these pupils is increased on an average by about three-quarters of an hour daily—no slight addition—by their private work ; but even if we disregard private work, a large proportion of the boys, as has been shown, would still be found to have longer hours than are allowed by the standard for perfectly healthy children. Nor, from a pedagogic point of view, can it be held to be right for the schools to absorb so much of their pupils' time that none is practically left for other teaching, where such may be thought desirable.

Private lessons in dancing and gymnastics are not included in the time devoted to extra work, as both these exercises tend to strengthen the body. The table shows that 621 (20 per cent of the total number of pupils) have dancing lessons, while only 86 (2·4 per cent) receive private instruction in gymnastics, including riding and fencing. This is in characteristic and striking contrast to the numbers who have music lessons, in spite of the much more beneficial results which would accrue to many of these anæmic, delicate children from gymnastics and bodily exercise.

Table XII. shows how many pupils find difficulty in keeping up with their class, and the subjects in which this is particularly the case. As already mentioned in the Introduction, the results here are somewhat uncertain, and the large proportion of non-returns still further diminishes their value. It is, however, curious to note how many pupils in the rhetorical section have difficulty with mathematics, and in the natural science section with Latin. This may be taken to show how necessary and practical is the division between these two branches of education.

TABLE XII.

CLASS.	No. of Boys who have *no* difficulty in keeping up with Class.	No. of Boys who have difficulty in keeping up with Class in :—												Non-returned.
		All Subjects.	Danish Composition.	German.	French.	English.	Latin.	Greek.	Old Scandinavian History.	History.	Geography.	Arithmetic and Mathematics.	Natural History.	
1st Mixed . . .	58	5	...	...	...	...	...	...	...	...	...	2	...	96
2d do. . . .	123	17	1	...	...	...	...	...	...	...	...	6	...	61
3d do. . . .	173	38	4	2	...	...	...	...	...	3	7	19	...	56
4th do. . . .	210	41	4	1	...	1	...	...	...	9	10	26	3	65
5th do. . . .	188	39	15	9	6	12	...	...	...	11	9	37	3	66
6th do. . . .	173	42	11	6	20	8	...	...	...	11	5	15	2	67
TOTAL . . .	925	182	35	18	26	21	...	...	...	34	31	105	8	411
1st Modern . . .	48	22	5	8	17	6	...	...	...	13	4	24	2	35
2d do. . . .	76	15	3	18	16	5	...	...	...	3	10	54	1	22
3d do. . . .	30	9	4	17	5	2	...	...	...	3	...	28	2	23
4th do. . . .	16	6	7	8	...	...	...	...	...	1	1	15	5	15
TOTAL . . .	170	52	19	51	38	13	...	...	...	20	15	121	10	95
1st Classical . .	128	22	2	2	2	2	8	...	...	3	1	30	5	46
2d do. . .	91	9	1	3	6	...	28	...	...	...	...	32	...	32
3d do. . .	67	9	2	...	...	1	13	5	...	...	1	19	2	23
4th do. . .	51	3	...	1	...	1	9	4	...	1	...	12	1	15
5th do. . .	26	15	1	...	2	...	7	2	9	2	...	...	3	14
6th do. . .	25	5	3	...	2	...	3	1	...	3	...	...	5	10
TOTAL . . .	388	63	9	6	12	4	68	12	9	9	2	93	16	140
3d Natural Science	12	1	...	...	1	...	9	...	...	...	...	...	...	9
4th do.	4	...	...	...	...	...	9	...	...	...	...	1	1	2
5th do.	15	2	1	...	...	...	...	...	...	1	...	...	...	5
6th do.	12	...	2	...	...	...	...	...	...	1	...	1	...	...
TOTAL . . .	43	3	3	...	1	...	18	...	...	2	...	2	1	16

My reason for thus strongly emphasising the influence of school life upon the health of children has been partly because I believe it to be very considerable, and partly because the existing evils can be diminished to a great extent when once their seriousness is recognised. But it would be most unjust to impute to the schools the entire blame for the unsatisfactory state of health of the pupils attending them ; the large number of sickly children found in the lowest classes shows clearly how predisposed the children are to divers complaints and diseases. Besides this the domestic conditions under which even high-class school children live are in many cases not so favourable to their natural development and vigorous health as they could and should be. Many influences have to be considered, and it is difficult to ascribe to each one its due share in the production of the evils indicated. Thus, with respect to the hours of work, it is of importance that the pupils should have the necessary quiet for study without being disturbed by brothers and sisters, or having their attention dissipated by too much gaiety; also that they should have some guidance in their home

F

preparation, for many, especially young children, understand but imperfectly how to work by themselves until after some considerable experience.

The nourishment supplied to the children under consideration in this inquiry may be taken to be as good as is ever given to children in our country, though hardly as substantial as it ought to be. School children with us do not generally get their dinner until late in the afternoon; and until dinner they subsist all day on sandwiches, an article of food which, I think, enjoys too prominent a place in our dietary. It would decidedly be a great boon if it became customary to give children a good substantial meal in the morning in place of the cup of tea now generally indulged in before going to school, and which, along with a few sandwiches hastily devoured during the intervals between classes, is all the food that many school children get before their late dinner.

There can be no doubt that, next to good wholesome nourishment, a sufficient quantity of rest after hard mental toil ranks as most essential to the preservation of health. It is not so easy to state precisely how much sleep is necessary at different ages, but all will agree that on the whole children require plenty of sleep, considerably more than adults. A sufficiency of sleep is more par- ticularly needed by children doing hard brain work, which is certainly the most exhausting form of labour, so that mind and body may have time to recruit. Abundance of sleep is more than ever requisite when the development of the body is not sufficiently provided for at the same time by physical exercise. At what hours the pupils in the different classes go to bed, and how many hours' sleep they get, will be seen from the fol- lowing table.

TABLE XIII.

CLASS.	In Bed at	No. of hours of Sleep.	CLASS.	In Bed at	No. of hours of Sleep.
1st Mixed .	8·0 o'clk.	10·9	1st Classical (*Both Sections*)	9·4 o'clk.	9·3
2d ,, .	8·1 ,,	10·7	2d ,,	9·6 ,,	9·2
3d ,, .	8·4 ,,	10·4	3d ,,	9·9 ,,	8·8
4th ,, .	8·7 ,,	10·1	4th ,,	10·3 ,,	8·4
5th ,, .	8·9 ,,	9·9	5th ,,	10·9 ,,	7·9
6th ,, .	9·2 ,,	9·6	6th ,,	11·2 ,,	7·9
1st Modern .	9·6 o'clk.	9·3			
2d ,, .	9·7 ,,	9·0			
3d ,, .	9·9 ,,	8·9			
4th ,, .	10·1 ,,	8·7			

Whereas the table shows the average returned
for each class, and which, at least as far as the
younger classes are concerned, may be said to be
satisfactory, still there is a considerable number
who manifestly do not get enough of sleep.

I have drawn up a table showing the number
of boys who do not get sufficient rest, and the
amount of sleep which I regard as insufficient for
children at the respective ages enumerated.

TABLE XIV.

CLASSES.	No. of hrs'. sleep.	No. of Children	Percentage.
Mixed 1–3	9·0	27	...
,, 4–6	8·5	42	4
Modern 1–4	8·0	63	12
Classical 1–4	8·0	97	...
,, 5–6	7·5	55	18
TOTAL		284	9

Mention is, of course, only made here of those who
are reported as getting too little sleep, but there
must be many more boys who are often allowed to
remain up much past their usual bedtime, though

the forms do not divulge this irregularity. As might have been expected, it is more particularly amongst the older boys that cases of insufficiency of sleep are most frequent, and of these there are many who sit up far too late, it being no uncommon thing for some of them to protract their studies till midnight or even till one in the morning.

Taking the average work done by the pupils of the various classes, we naturally find that many fall short of this, while many, again, greatly exceed it ; and it is very interesting to see what is done in individual cases in the way of work. Thus, in the mixed classes, of the 73 boys working beyond the "normal" standard, 22 exceed it by as much as two hours, while 6 work over eleven hours a day, and such instances are even to be found among children between nine and ten years old. In several forms it is stated that boys have to practise music for one and a half to two hours a day. So, too, there are some little fellows from eight to nine years old who only go to bed at eleven o'clock. In the modern department there are 68 boys and in the classical 174 who work at least one hour over and

above the "normal" limit, and of these, 41 moderns
and 74 classicals thus exceed in school work alone.
Even in the youngest classes there are one or two
boys who do twelve hours' work daily, including,
however, extra work ; in the oldest classes this is
by no means unusual, there being no less than 10
boys in the fifth classical form who work their
twelve hours a day. A few scholars even attain to
thirteen and fourteen hours of work daily, but in
these cases it is stated that they are far behind in
one or two subjects, and have therefore to make
special exertions. That such an enormous amount
of daily work performed by immature beings can
fail in the long run to affect the health is incred-
ible, and it is perhaps still more doubtful whether
the advantages to be gained by such intemperate
industry can in any degree outweigh its inevitable
injurious consequences ; it is more probable that
the boy thus overtasked at last ceases to learn
anything at all.

Only in a very few cases probably have the
school authorities been aware of the actual extent
of the work entailed by their requirements ; for,
where so much labour is necessary, the pupil ought

certainly either to diminish his studies or else
remain a year longer in the class; and some
arrangement of this kind would doubtless have
been insisted on in many cases had the preceptors
been cognisant of the weight of the load of home
work which their zeal was imposing. It is absolutely and cruelly wrong to let any boy proceed
with such exhausting work. I know, too, of cases
in which, after having seen from my schedules
how long certain boys had to work, and after
having convinced itself of the truth of the statements made, the school has conferred with the
parents, and by arrangement with them curtailed
the work and caused the pupil to remain another
year in the same class. This is very proper,
and shows of what consequence it is for the
school authorities to know exactly how long the
boys work at home. When the schoolmaster
hears of a pupil working longer than is warrant-
able in proportion to his age and strength, it is
undoubtedly his duty to call the parents' attention to the fact, and in conjunction with them to
take the necessary steps to bring about a more
reasonable state of things. In German school pro-

spectuses I have seen earnest appeals to parents and guardians to give instant notice to the school if they consider that the pupil is forced to spend more time upon his home preparation than is reasonable. In the Swedish high schools the pupils have to state, twice a year, how much time they devote to home work ; and if, as may be expected, this rule is enforced in our country, let us hope that, in the event of a similar inquiry being made, we may not discover so many abnormal conditions as I have here shown to exist. The mere fact of calling attention to these points is sure to secure some good results.

In exceptional cases, such as I have quoted above, it is more especially the parents and guardians upon whom the responsibility rests. When the children have already enough to do with their school tasks they ought not to be saddled with extra work, and I must here specially make mention of music lessons, which undoubtedly form the addition to the daily toil which can best be omitted. Many boys practise music for from one and a half to two hours a day. When a child gives proof of any special musical talent, that ought of course to be cultivated, but for the most part the music lesson is only a burden which heavily oppresses the already overloaded pupil and prevents him from getting as much out-door exercise as he ought to have. There are probably but few boys who keep up their music when they grow older, so as to derive any real benefit from it.

CHAPTER III.

GIRLS' SCHOOLS.

I HAVE collected statistics from ten girls' schools, all of them belonging to the largest and best class of Girls' High Schools in Copenhagen. There being no legal regulations as to the amount of work to be done in girls' schools, nor any exit examinations as in the case of boys' schools, the headmistresses have it in their own power to prescribe what work they think best, and to arrange the classes at their own discretion. In the main there is probably but little difference between the work done in the various girls' schools, so that for all practical purposes they may be taken to be upon an equal footing. Like the boys, the girls included in this inquiry belong to the well-to-do upper classes in town, and live under the best external conditions. Owing to the power of the headmistresses to organise their schools as they think proper, so that the classes in the various schools do not correspond, it has been impossible for me to arrange the girls by class, as in the case of the boys' schools. I have therefore had to classify them according to age, whereby, no doubt, an equally good review is obtained, though certainly this process has been much more troublesome. In all other respects the statistics have been arranged in exactly the same manner as in the case of the boys' schools.

Altogether 1211 girls, between the ages of five and sixteen, have been examined. Of these there were—healthy 644, sickly 477, non-returned 90. The percentages being—healthy 53·1, sickly 39·4, non-returned 7·5.

The percentage of sickly is much greater than in the boys' schools, in which it will be recollected the percentages were—healthy 60·5, sickly 31·1, non-returned 8·4, and this result corresponds with the common experience that girls are on the whole more delicate than boys.

The state of health of the girls at different ages is clearly shown by the curves on Chart III. and by Table XV. The black line in the Chart indicates the healthy, the dotted one the sickly, and the lowest the non-returned. The percentage of sickly girls rises rapidly in the first three years from 12·7 to 32 per cent, while the percentage of healthy declines inversely from 79·7 to 59·4. Thus in the third school year the results are about the same as in the boys' schools, and remain pretty stationary until the eleventh year, when a sudden rise brings the percentage of sickly almost up to that of the healthy children. Between the ages of twelve and sixteen the number of sickly girls increases until it exceeds that of healthy by 10 per cent, except at the age of fourteen, where the figures are equal. The non-returns remain almost unvaryingly at 7 per cent until the very end, at the age of sixteen, when the health column is filled up in every case, with the result that there is a sudden rise in the percentage of sickly, without any corresponding fall in the percentage of healthy cases. The number of girls in each age-section, with the exception of the sixth and highest ones, is on an average 120 or more, and is thus large enough to justify us in regarding the results as trustworthy. Sickness among schoolgirls here shows itself unmistakably to be so great that we must put aside all illusions and openly confess that the present generation of young girls is weakly, anæmic, and nervous to an extraordinary degree. Our school-girls are alarmingly far from being as healthy and strong as they should be, especially when it is remembered that those here dealt with belong socially to the best class in Copenhagen.

If, as in the boys' schools, we regard the first two years as a criterion of the state of health at the commencement of the process of education we get the following percentages :—healthy 71·0, sickly 22·0, non-returned 7·0.

Thus girls have a strong predisposition to various diseases to start with, and it is therefore easy to understand that school routine and private tuition, which must affect girls even more potently than boys, soon induce various diseases, and especially anæmia, to assert themselves more strongly than before. More particularly during the years of puberty does sickness prevail to a great extent, at least one-half of the pupils being at this period more or less debilitated or ill. It is universally acknowledged that the period of puberty is at least as momentous an epoch in the development of a young girl as it is in that of a boy ; but I am not in possession of such statistics relating to girls as Dr. Kotelmann furnishes with reference to the rate of growth of boys at this time, and cannot therefore give detailed proof of a girl's growth during this stage of evolution. My investigation shows this much however, that a sad number of young girls of fifteen and sixteen years of age, on leaving school, suffer from anæmia, nervousness, and headache—the complaints which specially characterise our time. If we take the numbers in the oldest classes as an indication of the state of health on leaving school, we get—out of 78 pupils—healthy 32, sickly 41, non-returned 5. Percentages—healthy 41, sickly 53, non-returned 6.

There is thus a considerable preponderance of sickly, which is still further emphasised by a comparison with the two youngest classes (*vide* Table XV.). It is impossible but that so much sickliness for four or five years—and that, too, at a period when the whole body should be in a state of active nutrition—must exert a great influence upon the whole future physical develop-

ment of a girl, and it is therefore readily explained how in widely different ranks of life we
meet with so many weakly women. The health
of many a girl receives at this period an injury
the effects of which are never completely surmounted. This is of most serious consequence in
the case of the numerous young girls who, almost
immediately after leaving school, without having
time to recover their strength, are obliged to prepare for pass-examinations as teachers or to enter
upon a commercial training. The work demanded
of them in such cases is very arduous, and it is probably a rare thing to find among those engaged in
these callings a really strong and healthy young
woman ; the great majority suffer very much from
chronic anæmia and nervousness. The work is
often of a highly oppressive description, and
interferes with appetite and sleep.

That school life, and indeed the whole system
of educating young girls at present in vogue in
our country, are largely responsible for this sad
state of things can scarcely be doubted. We
must some time or other face this truth boldly
before any real improvement can be secured.

There are, of course, headmasters and mistresses
who perceive that the state of health of their pupils
is bad, but these are comparatively few ; and I have
so often heard it said, under circumstances where
such a complacent pronouncement was only too
obviously incorrect, " Well, fortunately in our
school the health is really very good," that I feel
fully justified in saying that many teachers are
quite blind to, or incapable of judging of, the
health of their scholars. I have heard the above
assertion boldly made in girls' schools which this
investigation has proved to have 40 per cent of
sickly scholars, and in boys' schools in which there
were up to 35 per cent of sickly scholars, that is to
say in schools which have an unusually high percentage of sickly inmates. It may perhaps be
argued against me that the statements received from
parents as to the enfeeblement of health in children
are exaggerated. The reverse is, however, the
case. I have received intimations from some
schools to the effect that several children who, in
the opinion of the school, are weak and sickly
have not been entered as such upon the schedules,
the health column being either left blank or the

children returned as healthy. The headmaster of one large boys' school in particular has in many cases expressed his opinion, in the column for remarks by the school, as to the health of the children, and thereby supplemented the statement from home in such a manner as to warrant me in classifying as sickly several children who would not otherwise have appeared in that group. When, for example, "cough" has been set down in the health column, without any further statement as to whether it was an acute casual catarrh or a chronic affection of the chest, I have classified the child as non-returned ; when, however, the school adds "often absent on account of complaint," this remark completely supplements the insufficient information on the part of the parents.

A still better proof is obtained from the curves of Chart I., which represents the state of health in boys' schools. From the third to the sixth classical form the line indicating the percentage of "healthy" remains almost at the same figure throughout, while the line which registers the percentage of "sickly" takes a sudden leap upwards in the fifth classical form and falls as rapidly in the

sixth. If we compare this with the line of
"non-returns" we find that the large percentage
of sickly children in the fifth classical form is due
to the fact that there are hardly any non-returns
(only 1·3 per cent), whereas the rapid decline in
the sixth form is accounted for by the large
number of non-returns in that class (nearly 14
per cent). We find the same relation in the
third and fourth modern forms; the percentage
of healthy children hardly varies from the second
class upwards, while that of the sickly falls
from 30 to 23 per cent, simultaneously with the
percentage of non-returns in these classes from
9 to 18. On the girls' chart exactly the same
thing takes place in the sixteenth year. Thus
it invariably happens that a decrease in the percentage of non-returns is accompanied by a
proportional increase in the number of sickly,
and *vice versa*, while the percentage of healthy
is not materially affected by the fluctuation of the
non-returns. Indeed the returns of "healthies"
are the most correct and reliable, whereas the
percentage of "non-returns" properly ought to be
added to that of the "sicklies." When we reflect,

too, that all these returns have been made in the autumn—a couple of months after the summer holidays—and at a time when, as a matter of fact, the health of the community at large is better. than at any other season ; and that last year, when the investigation was made, we were exempt from epidemics such as measles or scarlet fever, which might have confused the returns ; and, finally, that a minute examination of the eyesight is absolutely wanting, it must be decidedly maintained that, in spite of the excessively high per- centage of sickly we have obtained, it must be regarded as a minimum in the case of the girls' as well as the boys' schools.

Particulars as to the various complaints from which Danish schoolgirls suffer are given on Table XV. The most prevalent ones are clearly seen to be anæmia, nervousness, and headache, and up to the fourteenth year scrofula. In the oldest classes one of the most common complaints is also headaches. Four per cent of the total number of girls are seen to be suffering from curvature of the spine—no small proportion considering that probably only the worst cases are

TABLE XV.

Ages.	Healthy.	Anæmia.	Scrofula.	Nervousness.	Headaches.	Bleeding at the Nose.	Curvature of the Spine.	Diseases of the Eye.	Other Complaints.	Casual Complaints.	Total Sickly.	Non-returned.	Healthy. (Per cent)	Sickly. (Per cent)	Non-returned. (Per cent)
5-6 Years	63	2	3	3	1	:	:	1	:	:	10	6	79·7	12·7	7·6
7 ,,	66	7	8	7	2	3	1	1	2	2	30	7	64·1	29·1	6·8
8 ,,	78	13	9	8	9	2	1	2	6	2	42	11	59·4	32·0	8·6
9 ,,	83	22	10	7	12	1	2	1	2	1	46	13	58·5	32·3	9·2
10 ,,	77	14	12	9	10	2	2	4	1	:	41	10	60·2	32·0	7·8
11 ,,	76	33	17	13	15	5	4	3	5	4	70	8	49·4	45·5	5·1
12 ,,	60	31	17	12	26	3	5	2	5	:	75	11	41·1	51·4	7·5
13 ,,	49	25	15	6	20	3	6	3	6	:	62	9	40·8	51·7	7·5
14 ,,	60	28	14	7	18	3	3	5	4	:	60	10	46·2	46·2	7·6
15 ,,	27	17	2	6	18	3	1	:	1	:	33	5	41·5	50·8	7·7
16 ,,	5	5	1	1	6	:	1	:	:	:	8	:	39·0	61·0	:
Total	644	197	108	79	137	25	26	22	32	9	477	90	53·1	39·4	7·5
Per cent	...	31	17	12	22	4	4	4	5	1	...	...	...	...	...
5-7 Hrs	129	9	11	10	3	3	1	2	2	2	40	13	71·0	22·0	7·0
Per cent	...	21	25	23	7	7	2	5	5	5	...	...	...	...	...
15-16 Years	32	22	3	7	24	3	2	:	1	:	41	5	41·0	53·0	6·0
Per cent	...	35	5	11	39	5	3	:	2	:	...	...	...	...	...

Total—635 cases of Sickness among 477 Children.

reported here. The percentage of sickly varies from 33, which is the lowest, to 45, which is the highest percentage in any school.

Hours of Work at different Ages.

As previously mentioned, private tuition plays an even more important part in the case of girls' than in that of boys' schools, as a much larger proportion of girls (62 per cent) take private lessons. This is more particularly the case after the tenth year, when from 75 to 92 per cent of the girls have extra work. On Chart IV. I have indicated the work hours by two lines—the lower giving the number of hours of school work daily, and the upper the number of hours of daily work including private tuition. Both lines rise, on the whole, pretty equally, the average increase due to private work being one hour *per diem*. There is a gradual addition of about three-tenths of an hour for each year, except from the fourteenth to the sixteenth year, when no increase of importance takes place. Eight hours a day is in no case reached through school work alone, but as private tuition undoubtedly is the rule after the tenth year the actual

work time is increased by one hour. Thus at
the age of eleven the girls have on an average eight
hours of work, and between the ages of fourteen
and sixteen almost nine hours daily (*vide* Table
XVI.), so that the limit fixed for boys in perfect
health is thus slightly exceeded by girls of from
fourteen to fifteen years of age.

I will not go the length of asserting that, as
a rule, girls are not able for as much work as
boys; though, for my part, I do not think they are.
It is true that their sewing lessons afford them
a change from mental work which boys do not
enjoy, but they are compelled none the less to sit
still during these and in a stooping position—
while, on the other hand, the counteracting effect
which gymnastics exert is less pronounced in
their case; the girls in most of the classes have
only an hour and a half of gymnastics weekly, and
in two of the schools this healthy exercise forms
no part of the programme whatever.

It is certain, therefore, that girls have a great
deal of work—far more than they should have—
particularly when one reflects that the majority
of them, as has been shown, are not normally

TABLE XVI.

Ages.	Number of Pupils.	Weekly — Number of Hours at School.	Languages.	Written Exercises.	Singing.	Drawing.	Writing.	Sewing, etc.	Gymnastics.	Total.	Daily — Sewing, etc.	School Work.	School, plus Extra Work.	Class 1	Class 2	Class 3	Private Tuition — Number of Pupils.	Percentage.	Music.	Other Subjects.	Dancing.
5-6 Years	79	24-30	0- 4	...	0·1	0·2	0·6	4-10	0·3	8-16	0·7	4·8	6·6	5·1	4·6	5·1	4	5	3	1	14
7 do.	103	24-30	0- 5	0·1	0·1	0·2	0·6	4-10	0·3	8-16	1·1	5·4	6·3	5·6	5·2	5·6	13	12	13	..	27
8 do.	131	24-36	0- 7	0·2	0·1	0·2	0·6	3-10	0·3	7-16	1·2	5·8	6·5	5·9	5·6	5·9	44	34	44	..	36
9 do.	142	26-36	3-10	0·3	0·1	0·2	1·4	3-10	0·3	7-16	1·6	6·4	7·3	6·4	6·4	6·5	78	55	71	7	50
10 do.	128	30-36	4-10	0·3	0·1	0·2	1·3	3- 7	0·3	6-13	1·9	6·7	7·7	6·8	6·5	7·1	96	75	91	5	35
11 do.	154	30-36	4-10	0·4·5	1	0·2	1·3	3- 6	0·3	6-12	2·1	7·1	8·1	6·9	7·2	7·3	111	75	107	4	44
12 do.	146	30-36	4-10	0·4·5	1	0·2	1·3	3- 6	0·3	6-12	2·4	7·4	8·3	7·2	7·6	7·6	129	88	117	12	36
13 do.	120	30-33	5-11	0·4·5	0·1	0·2	1·3	3- 6	0·2	7-12	2·5	7·5	8·6	7·5	7·4	7·8	100	83	93	7	31
14 do.	130	30-33	4-11	1·4	0·1	0·2	1·3	3- 6	0·2	7-12	2·8	7·9	8·9	7·7	8·0	7·9	110	85	101	9	26
15 do.	65	30-33	6-11	1·4	0·1	0·2	1·3	3- 5	0·2	7-10	2·8	7·8	9·1	7·6	8·0	7·8	60	92	59	1	9
16 do.	13	30-32	6-10	2·4	0·1	0·2	1·3	3- 5	0·2	7-10	3·1	8·0	8·8	8·5	7·7	8·7	8	58	8	..	4
Total	1211																753		707	46	312
Percentage of Total Number of Pupils																	62·2	62·2	58·4	3·8	26·0
Percentage of Extra Work																	...	...	93	7	...

healthy, but delicate and anæmic, requiring to be strengthened in every possible way. Instead of this, however, they are daily permitted to do sedentary and exhausting work for eight or nine hours, and I am guilty of no exaggeration in saying that in my practice, when I have advised parents to see that their children take a proper walk every day, I have almost invariably been met with the reply, "You really mustn't expect that; the children have no time for it." This answer is to a certain extent true. Let us consider for a moment how a young girl of fourteen, with nine hours of daily work, spends her day. At nine o'clock, after having partaken of a cup of tea and some plain bread and butter, she goes to school, where she remains until two or three o'clock. Thence she proceeds to her music lesson, or goes home to practise for an hour, and sometimes for two hours; then comes dinner, and after that, at five or half-past, she sets to work at preparation, which occupies her for three hours or more—in fact, until tea-time. How can she then find time for a walk, especially in winter when the days are short? It is a matter to be thankful for if she has some little distance to go to school, and can in that way get a daily walk, which is indeed the limit of the muscular exercise now enjoyed by many young girls in Denmark. The performance of household work of any kind by schoolgirls is a thing rarely, if ever, heard of. If they have any spare time at all it is generally spent in sewing or reading a novel. The above is the case in very many places, though, of course, there are exceptions. With the predisposition of the present generation to anæmia and nervousness a sedentary life like this cannot fail to produce its effects, and the tremendous number of sickly cases during the years of puberty is a proof of this. The blame does not rest on the school system alone, but quite as much upon the whole system of educating young girls at the present day.

The hours of work at the various ages are given in Table XVI. Here, too, the hours vary so much in the different schools that it has been impossible to give reliable averages.

In all, 753 girls receive private tuition. It is for the most part after the tenth year that extra work becomes common. 707 have music lessons (which is 93 per cent of those having private tuition), while only 7 per cent receive instruction in other subjects—chiefly languages. It is thus almost entirely music lessons with which we have to deal here, and perhaps a modest doubt may be raised as to whether so many girls really have a special aptitude for music, and whether to the majority of them it is not just a vexation— a thing from which they will derive neither profit nor pleasure in after life, but which, at the period when school claims so much of their time and energy, is actually distressing and injurious to them. The fact that one-third of the total number of girls devote more than six hours a week to music shows that it is often a considerable addition to the daily work. Many girls practise nine hours, and not a few from twelve to sixteen hours a week, and music lessons are certainly as wearying and exhausting as any other kind of enforced work.

As in the case of the boys' schools, I have made out a table showing how many girls have "hard work," for which purpose I have employed the same standard as for the boys. The result is as follows :—

TABLE XVII.

AGES.	NORMAL WORK. No. of Hours.	NORMAL WORK. No. of Pupils.	Percentage.	HARD WORK. No. of Pupils.	Percentage.	School Work.	Extra Wk.	NON-RETURNED. No. of Pupils.	Percentage.
5-6 Years	6	72	91·1	5	6·4	2	3	2	2·5
7 do.	6	74	71·8	26	25·2	21			3·
8 do.	7·3	118	90·1	11	8·4	5			1·
9 do.	7·5	114	80·3	27	19·0	10	1		0·
10 do.	7·8	78	60·9	47	36·7	18	2		2·
11 do.	8	97	63·0	54	35·1	10	4		1·
12 do.	8·3	82	56·2	60	41·1	14	4		2·
13 do.	8·5	74	61·7	44	36·7	13	3		1·
14 do.	8·8	67	51·5	61	47·0	23	3		1·
15 do.	9	36	55·4	27	41·5	1	26		3·
16 do.	9	9	69·2	4	30·8	1	3	...	...
Total		821	67·8	366	30·2	118	248	24	2·0
Percentage . .		...	...	...	...	32	68	...	...

Of the total number of girls no less than 30 per cent have "hard work," i.e. almost one-third, and chiefly at the ages of twelve, fourteen, and fifteen, in which sections the percentages are over 40. In the majority of cases (68 per cent) this is due to extra work, but in 32 per cent the limit is exceeded by school work alone. The relations between school and extra work are thus reversed as compared with the boys' schools, where, in the majority of cases, the excess was due to school work alone.

As in the boys' schools, no constant or regular difference is observable in the work hours of the clever, middling, or dull girls respectively (*vide* Table XVI.).

There are several girls too, who, like many of the boys, have to work far beyond the so-called "normal" time. As I have not come across any statement of the maximum number of hours during which girls should be allowed to work I have taken the same standard for them as for boys, although a lower one ought certainly to have been adopted. I do not think any one would fix a higher limit than this, and yet about one-third of the girls exceed it; indeed there are 97 girls (8 per cent of the whole) who work at least one hour beyond the "normal" time, 8 of them doing more than eleven hours' work, 4 twelve hours, and 2 working even between thirteen and fourteen hours daily. It is not surprising to find that the majority of these children are returned as sickly (the percentages being 37 healthy and 56 sickly, with 6 non-returned), but one cannot help wondering how their parents could have allowed them to go on struggling with such excessive work. In many cases the teachers have been ignorant of the inordinate burdens laid on their pupils, several of the children having as much as twelve hours of music lessons weekly, which, of course, are beyond the jurisdiction of the school. Even the medical men who have signed the forms cannot be supposed to have known before they did so how long the children worked, else they must surely have entered a protest against such a state of things. I shall quote one or two instances. One girl of fourteen spends 10½ hours daily at school and in preparation of school work, besides practising music for an hour, so that she has 11½ hours of daily work. According to the doctor's return she had a slight attack of inflammation of the brain about six months ago, and still suffers constantly from headaches; while it is expressly mentioned that there is some danger of the disease being brought on again by overwork. Another case is that of a girl of twelve, who is 5 hours at school, spends 6 hours daily in preparation, and practises 8 hours a week, giving a total of nearly 12½ hours of daily work.

Her doctor states in the return that she suffers from scrofula, nervous headache located in the forehead, heartburn, vomiting, diarrhœa at intervals, anæmia, and also that her right shoulder has a tendency to droop. The above returns are each signed by a medical man. I could add several cases of a similar nature, but the above are sufficient to show that we doctors must not forget to ascertain exactly how long our juvenile patients work, for we may often be greatly aided by the information which inquiries on this point will bring to light in discovering causes of sickness. As a rule, it would be well if parents would consult the doctor oftener than they do at present about the education of their children. Many children are now sent to school far earlier than their physical and mental development warrants, and this crying evil would be put a stop to were the advice of the family doctor systematically taken on all educational proceedings.

The average bedtime and number of hours of sleep of girls at each age are given in Table XVIII.

TABLE XVIII.

AGES.	In bed at	No. of hrs. of Sleep.	AGES.	In bed at	No. of hrs. of Sleep.
5-6 Years	7·8 o'clk.	11·1	12 Years	9·4 o'clk.	9·6
7 ,,	8·1 ,,	10·6	13 ,,	9·6 ,,	9·3
8 ,,	8·4 ,,	10·5	14 ,,	9·8 ,,	9·0
9 ,,	8·6 ,,	9·9	15 ,,	9·9 ,,	8·9
10 ,,	9·0 ,,	9·9	16 ,,	10·0 ,,	8·7
11 ,,	9·1 ,,	9·7			

If the children went to bed at the average hours stated, they might, on the whole, be supposed to get enough sleep. There are, however, many who get much less. Applying the same rule as we did for the boys we find that the following get too little rest :—

TABLE XIX.

AGES.	No. of hours of Sleep.	No. of Pupils.	Percentage.
7-9 Years	9·0	17	4
10-12 ,,	8·5	23	5
13-16 ,,	8·0	62	19
Total		102	8

Thus 8 per cent of the total number of girls get too little sleep, and in particular many amongst the older classes.

312 girls, or 26 per cent, take dancing lessons, which are pretty evenly distributed throughout all the age-sections, except the two oldest; only one or two have private lessons in gymnastics. The dancing lessons are not included in the time spent in private work.

TABLE XX.

AGES.	Have no difficulty in keeping up with the Class.	Have difficulty in keeping up the class in:—									Non-returned.
		Everything.	Danish Composition.	German.	French.	English.	History.	Geography.	Arithmetic.	Natural History.	
5-6 Years	48	3	...	...	...	...	...	...	1	...	26
7 ,,	61	7	...	...	...	...	...	...	1	...	32
8 ,,	82	8	1	1	1	...	3	2	...	...	34
9 ,,	85	18	1	1	2	2	6	5	2	...	24
10 ,,	80	12	3	1	4	...	8	3	3	2	17
11 ,,	91	19	3	1	8	6	9	4	6	1	14
12 ,,	76	15	5	3	8	9	10	3	5	...	15
13 ,,	61	24	3	6	7	1	7	3	5	...	8
14 ,,	69	23	5	1	9	3	6	3	6	4	8
15 ,,	33	9	1	4	6	1	3	...	6	3	4
16 ,,	6	2	1	1	2	...	2	2	...	...	1
Total	692	140	23	24	47	22	54	25	35	10	183

Table XX. shows how many children have difficulty with their work. These returns seem to have given some little trouble to prepare, and no less than 15 per cent of parents have altogether omitted to fill in this column. One thing only seems pretty clear, viz. that a comparatively large number find more or less difficulty in doing the work of the class.

A good many girls (53 or 54 per cent) have not taken all the subjects worked by their classes, one or more languages in particular having been omitted. It is a great advantage that this is allowed in girls' schools, and the system ought to be much more generally adopted, either when the child shows no turn for a particular subject or cannot stand as much work as the rest. In the boys' schools, in which an examination prescribed by law is the goal, this relief can only be afforded under very exceptional circumstances.

CHAPTER IV.

GENERAL CONCLUSIONS.

IF we now look back upon the results we have obtained in our inquiry into the condition of the children in Danish high schools, they appear truly sad and appalling, but, it may be asked, can these results be regarded as really reliable? To this I emphatically answer in the affirmative. They are as reliable as any information which is based upon a single inquiry can be. Knowing, as I do, that some people cast doubts upon the trustworthiness of the returns, and that these doubts have already been expressed in some quarters, I may perhaps (as this is, of course, an important point) be allowed to point out that the schedules have been filled in by the most intelligent and best informed portion of the population of Copenhagen, and that there is not the slightest ground for insinuating that cultivated and well-informed parents have not bestowed due care and reflection upon the answering of questions, to which they were in all earnestness urged to reply.

That amongst several thousand returns some mistakes and errors should not have crept in it could never occur to me to deny, and I know besides that one or two of the pupils have filled up the forms themselves without the knowledge of their parents, but such cases are quite exceptional, as I took occasion to point out in the introduction. The great majority of schedules are signed by the parents, who thus vouch for the correctness of the answers. The perfect regularity with which from class to class the work hours increase, and the hours of sleep decrease, tallies with what one might expect; nor is there a single detail in which the results take the form of an improbability. Looked at in the aggregate, the results all bear evidence of being genuine. There are no sudden leaps or bounds, no unexpected fluctuations, but a perfectly gradual development from the youngest to the oldest classes. Added to this,

my special request to the school teachers to mark
all statements which appeared to them doubtful
has been in most instances complied with, and
such statements have been reckoned amongst the
non-returns. The results for both boys' and
girls' schools correspond, too, with one another in
all important particulars in which the influences
at work are not totally different,—as is the case,
for example, with regard to the state of health in
the oldest classes. All the calculations have been
made as carefully and conscientiously as possible,
and the result of each accurately stated. As it
is the home work in particular which is supposed
to have been over-stated, I may be allowed just
to refer to the fact that it is shown to be even
more in several classes in the Swedish schools. I
maintain, therefore, that my results must be considered absolutely reliable until clear proof to the
contrary can be adduced; the vague arguments of
men who perhaps have had no opportunity of
seeing for themselves how the questions have been
answered cannot be held to carry any weight.

This investigation has proved the existence
in boys' schools of so great a number of delicate

sickly children, that our school authorities ought most unquestionably to have regard to this fact in fixing the hours and standards of work, which as they now stand, even in the case of perfectly sound and healthy children, must be regarded as excessive. This applies even more forcibly to girls' schools, in the higher classes of which sickliness prevails to such an extent that the sickly preponderate over the healthy children ; there are classes in which the number of sickly girls exceeds 70 per cent. It is thus perfectly certain that in boys' and girls' schools alike the influence of school work prejudicially affects the children's physical development. This is clearly shown by the considerably larger percentage of healthy children in the lowest classes ; as the school work increases, so does the sickliness, and of the young lads and girls who leave school a great number do so with constitutions more or less impaired and weakened — some of them to such an extent that they never get over the bad effects of their early training. Many a young fellow only recovers his health after his time of service in the army, which is favourable to his bodily development; but this advantage is not given to all young men, many students, in particular, being rejected on account of shortsightedness.

And what is gained by all this? Are the results with respect to the young people's attainments and mental grasp so brilliant that they counterbalance the injury which their bodily growth and vigour have sustained? I do not think any one will maintain that they are. On the contrary, we hear constantly, on all hands, loud complaints of the meagreness of the mental attainments of our youth—boys as well as girls. Among the many persons with whom I have spoken about these matters I have not yet met one individual who has expressed himself as fully satisfied with the results of the training given in our schools. I have heard many severe criticisms of that training by men and women whose position entitled them to an opinion on the subject.

I have also frequently heard thoughtful and competent men express their conviction that many of our young students lack the mental ripeness and development which are necessary in order that they may pursue with full advantage their studies at the university. I have had no opportunity of personally making any observations in this matter, and can only repeat what more experienced men have told me, but the same comment has been made in other countries. Professor Kjelberg of Upsala expresses himself very decidedly to the same effect, and from Germany come similar complaints. Besides, it is most unlikely that ten to eleven hours of daily school work for several years should tend to develop a mature mind and a strong independent character. The latter is much more likely to become enfeebled by the ceaseless daily grinding at the prescribed tasks, which all tend to check any independent development. Many young men declare, too, that their memories have been seriously weakened. I shall not enter further into these questions, which rather fall within the province of the pedagogues, to whose careful consideration I commend them.

In the girls' schools the state of health is even worse ; so deplorable a result as my investigations have revealed cannot fail to open the eyes of all to the necessity of making some change in the present system of educating girls. That this was fully recognised on the part of teachers themselves as far back as 1872, is seen from the proposal then made by Miss Zahle. In a little treatise *On the Culture of Women in Denmark* Miss Zahle suggested that the period of education for girls should be extended to their eighteenth or nineteenth year, and also that the school work proper should be considerably diminished from the thirteenth to the fifteenth year ; these years should, she urged, be spent chiefly in a manner far more calculated to develop the body than they now are, and the girl should only receive as much teaching as might suffice to keep up what she had previously learned. This is certainly sound advice ; I hope it may be acted upon and prove itself practically useful.

The very one-sided culture which both boys and girls have hitherto received in this country has unhappily afforded painful demonstration of the inevitable consequences of neglecting the physical development, the care of which must rank in future as a far more important feature of education from early infancy up to manhood than it has yet done. The nervous and anæmic young people of the present day need much more con-

siderate treatment than has hitherto been accorded
to them if there is to be any prospect of de-
riving from them future generations physically
and mentally strong. I do not mean to say that
a child should not have a thoroughly good education, but he must be spared all unnecessary
burdens, and must be physically strengthened
and developed, so that he may be enabled to
throw off the general weakness from which the
present generation suffers. In order to attain this
end certain duties must be undertaken, and I
now propose to glance at some of them, especially
those incumbent upon the schools.

The chief characteristics of the last decade are
the enormous strides in natural science and the
immense development of all mechanical appliances
—machines of all kinds, railways, telegraphs, etc.
But with their general use has arisen a hitherto
almost unknown state of restlessness and competition, in which he who cannot keep up must
either succumb or be out-distanced. Simultaneously, personal requirements have grown in
number and extent, while the desire for luxury
and enjoyment has increased enormously and

become exceedingly peremptory in its demands. Everything and everybody is impelled onwards; there is no rest or breathing time either for the individual or for the general community. The consequence is that large numbers suffer from mental and bodily over-exertion and exhaustion. This is certainly a chief cause of the immense growth of anæmia and nervousness, which is so disastrous to the present generation. It is asserted from various quarters that as nervousness becomes more common mental diseases too are greatly on the increase; Dr. Hasse has even gone the length of instancing certain phases of insanity which he ascribes directly to overpressure in schools.

The nervous person is far less truly energetic, and is less able to endure sorrow and misfortune, than the man of stable temperament; he is easily affected by trifles, and becomes irritable and capricious—in short, loses all that mental equilibrium and physical endurance which a healthy man possesses. Instead of a hearty and natural enjoyment of the blessings of life a morbid craving for sensuous pleasure asserts its dominion over him, for an enfeebled nervous system requires constant stimulation. Women are most quickly affected, because they have, as a rule, a smaller stock of physical strength than men. Many a woman who has to support herself by her own efforts suffers from this anæmic nervous state; she is never quite well, never happy and contented, and is often obliged to give up the work she has undertaken because her bodily strength fails her. And as regards the married woman, who has a house and children to look after, we all know how difficult it often is for her to fulfil the important duties which devolve upon her—not so much from want of will as from want of strength! We all know how often a home under the guardianship of a woman thus enfeebled gradually exchanges its air of happiness and contentment for one of gloom and carelessness! The children's training suffers in consequence sorely; on the one hand they are petted by the anxious mother, who is afraid of the slightest cold in the head, and therefore wraps them up in greatcoats and comforters, and forbids them to go out if there happens to be the least wind; while on the other hand, when in the house, they are not allowed to stir lest they should

make a noise, but are enjoined to sit still with a
book in their hands, or engaged in some other
quiet occupation because their mother cannot endure the exuberance and restlessness, which are
inseparable from sound and lively child life, where
the natural tendency is to do anything but sit
motionless in one place for any length of time.
The mother suffers from their noise; she is fatigued
by their restlessness, by their running about and
constant questions, and therefore she tries as far
as possible to repress them. Thus the children
are prevented both from romping outside and
from stirring at home; they are petted at one
moment and scolded without any justification the
next; their whole training is carried on without
proper consistency or earnest method. We doctors,
alas! have frequent opportunities of seeing ex-
amples of such treatment, and they are very often
due to the nervous character and weak health of
the parents, the mothers in particular.

To be "a little nervous," as it is termed, is
thus (except in cases of a slight and temporary
nature) not an insignificant disadvantage—it is a
real misfortune, a daily cross, and consequently

of much greater importance than is commonly supposed. Those who suffer from this nervous state, who feel themselves weak and void of energy, will admit the truth of my statement—that this condition of feebleness is a very serious and embarrassing factor in all relations of life.

Nervousness, which consists in a morbid susceptibility to all impressions, is, moreover, hereditary. In the case of children, who are born with a predisposition to nervousness, it depends greatly upon their environment whether this tendency be checked or developed, and here it is that training is of the greatest importance. Now what sort of training do the children of the better classes get? Is it one which is calculated to modify or intensify the natural predisposition of the child when that tends to nervousness? It is, as a rule, so one-sided as to aim only at the development of the mental faculties, and that, too, in such a manner that "to give a child a good education" is almost synonymous with cramming it with as much of as many subjects as possible. When our great aim should be to counteract any morbid tendency in the nervous system, we force on the mental work to excess, and thereby to a great extent weaken the child's entire physical constitution. He thus becomes less capable of carrying on the fight for existence, which proves far more arduous to him than it ever required to be. I do not mean to assert that we can entirely exempt ourselves from the perturbing influences, the restlessness and bustle which characterise our time and set their mark upon us all, but we ought to do far more than we have yet attempted to counteract their effects. To find out the proper means to do so should now be our task, and it is one which, of course, cannot be accomplished in a short time, but we ought not to delay setting about it, and we must all work together, with the object of securing a powerful and healthy race of men and women— self-reliant, strong in character and will.

I have shown in the foregoing pages that there is a large number of sickly children in our schools, and that the percentage increases with the work. The work, therefore, must be curtailed, especially in the boys' schools. How this relief can be brought about—whether by a reduction in the number of subjects (let it be remembered that five or six languages are taught in the rhetorical section), or by not exacting as much in the various subjects as is now done—must be a matter for pedagogues to decide; it must, however, be a real relief that is obtained, not merely a little ineffective lopping-off here and there. It is hardly fair, either, on the part of school teachers to claim of the child an exclusive right to his time. There is much which he ought to learn beyond what the school imposes upon him; if he has any special talent or tastes—music or drawing, for example—he should have time at his own disposal in which to cultivate them. He should be able to pursue privately any of his school studies which specially attract or interest him, and altogether have more opportunities of independent growth allowed him than he has hitherto had. Are there not many students who have so little knowledge of themselves, their own powers, tastes, and inclinations, that it is a mere matter of chance what course of study they take up when they go to the university? For this reason many a young man, after having wasted a year or two, often makes a complete change and begins upon a totally different career. Those wasted years might often have been saved had he had opportunities while at school of studying a little by himself, and thus of judging in what direction his talents and predilections lay.

It may also be possible that a wrong system of teaching is in many cases to blame, and that relief might be afforded by making some change therein. Schoolmasters are specialists nowadays, and each is perhaps rather too apt to regard his own subject as all-important, forgetting how much work of a different kind his pupils have to do besides. This point is specially mentioned in the Report of the Norwegian School Commission of 1867, and regarded by the Commission as the chief cause of the excessive work by which many of the Norwegian pupils have been oppressed. It is also very probable that insufficient attention is paid to the preparation of lessons in the school itself, as many children, especially among the younger ones, do not understand how to set about preparing their tasks without help; it is also possible that the hearing of lessons plays too conspicuous a part, and, further, the school time tables are often faultily arranged; but all these are purely pedagogic questions, which I merely take the liberty of mentioning. The main need, after all, is a considerable lightening of the work throughout the school curriculum, from the age of twelve at the least.

The other plan, that of keeping boys at school a year longer, which of course would be a considerable gain in time, is not advisable for many reasons. A lad of eighteen ought not, as a rule, to go to school any more. The pupils' societies in Germany, where nineteen is the age for leaving school, and the demoralisation they have introduced may serve as warnings to us in many ways. Dr. Pilger, who has given his special attention to the subject, expresses the following severe judgment on the German youth :—"It is a matter of fact that within the last few decades a considerable proportion of the youth at our high schools has mentally and morally degenerated to a great extent." He attributes the blame rather to home than to school influences, though others again hold the opposite opinion. We have hitherto enjoyed immunity from such evils, but we ought certainly to avoid taking any step which might be the means of introducing them.

With the girls' schools the case is different. It is possible that the work prescribed by them might be retained, with perhaps some slight modifications—two foreign languages, thoroughly taught, should be enough; but in that case the school education of girls must not, as now, terminate at the age of fourteen or fifteen; it must be continued till the seventeenth or eighteenth year at the least, i.e. until the girls arrive at the age when they begin to understand the meaning of intellectual work and to derive advantage from it. It is an extraordinary fact that in the girls' high schools (to which this inquiry has been exclusively confined) the majority leave school when only fourteen years old, the number of girls of fifteen years old being only half as large as that of girls of fourteen. A girl's education stops far too early. It is quite impossible that her intellectual culture can be complete at that age, or that she can have mastered those attainments which are expected of, and indispensable to her as a well-educated woman. On the other hand, a considerable abatement of work is necessary from the eleventh year for four years onwards. To continue in the same manner as hitherto, after it has been shown that there are more sickly than healthy girls between the ages of twelve and sixteen, would be absolutely indefensible. Miss Zahle's proposal to reduce the school work during these years ought certainly to be considered afresh.

Girls' schools have the great advantage of being exempt from law-prescribed examinations, for which a certain amount of work has to be done, and it is therefore in the power of every head-mistress to introduce the necessary measures of relief, and to arrange the instruction in such a manner as may best meet the needs of the children.

The main thing now is to make a beginning and set an example which would deserve imitation. A proper measure of reform would be as great a relief to the school as to the scholars ; the former could then carry out its functions comfortably, without having to hurry through everything, and there is no doubt that the attainments acquired, deliber-ately and thoroughly taught, would be better remembered than the acquirements now, hurriedly and superficially picked up.

Now that so much sickliness has been shown to exist in our schools the demand for good hygienic arrangements will surely be acknowledged to be a just one. As I have elsewhere had occasion to mention, we are very far behind in this respect in Denmark. As early as 1866 Professor Drachmann proved statistically how bad was the accommodation in the girls' schools in Copenhagen. Since then improvements have been effected in some schools, and in particular in several of those which have furnished me with information. But, in spite of Professor Drachmann's testimony, no general improvement has taken place in school accommodation ; indeed, in this respect we stand exactly at the same point as we did thirty years ago. In the last few years I have repeatedly come across schoolrooms (not, however, in any of the schools included in this inquiry) with less than 50 cubic feet of air for each child. The minimum of 70 cubic feet prescribed by law is ludicrously small from a hygienic point of view, but certainly nothing short of it should be for one moment tolerated. This is the only legal regulation we have on the subject of school hygiene. As I have elsewhere [1] criticised the defectiveness of our legis-

[1] *Berling's Gazette* (the Danish official daily paper), 1880, Nos. 212, 213.

lation on all questions relating to school hygiene I shall not again enter upon that topic here. That it is extremely difficult for our large schools, if dependent upon their own resources, to find really good accommodation is unfortunately true. The schools here examined have, as far as I have had opportunities of judging, on the whole pretty serviceable class-rooms, if not always quite as good as might be desired. Many of them have begun to adopt more suitable furniture, which must in time entirely supplant the old and faultily-constructed desks and forms. Those weak and anæmic children stand in great need of well-adjusted seats during their long school hours, otherwise they are apt to fall into a crooked stooping posture, which is not only unsightly as regards carriage but affects the natural growth and functions of all the internal organs; the stooping position is also very favourable to the development of shortsightedness.

As the more old-fashioned buildings do not admit of a proper system of ventilation, the class-rooms must be carefully aired, and—what is of the utmost importance—kept very clean; but in this respect our boys' schools leave much to be desired. The girls' schools are, as a rule, much more cleanly. It is no uncommon thing to come upon boys' schools in which the floors are only scrubbed four times a year; however lofty and well ventilated such rooms may be, the air can never be good if the floors are not kept scrupulously clean. It is in the power of every school to keep its premises clean; the smaller they are, the greater the necessity. Cleanliness, scrupulously enforced, is at the root of all hygiene; if that be neglected, other measures are of no avail. It would be a great boon if all the floors in our schools (as is prescribed by law in Sweden) were polished. Not only the floors, however, but the cupboards and desks, should be regularly washed and kept dusted; quantities of dust containing decomposed organic matter accumulate upon all objects, and in the cracks in the floors. The tramping of the children sets the dust in motion, and it is inhaled with every breath. Owing to this great want of cleanliness not only the children but the teachers suffer, and the hoarseness and chronic catarrh which so often trouble the latter are more often due to impure air than to the so much dreaded cooling down of the rooms by leaving the windows open during the intervals of school work. It is not the cold fresh air, which soon gets warm, but the hot and dusty air, loaded with germs, which is injurious. A small and badly-aired room, moreover, affects the work of the class; the powers of attention of the children are impaired, they get tired and have difficulty in following what they are taught, as every teacher will admit. An improvement in the hygienic arrangement is therefore as much to the advantage of the teacher as of the pupils. That the cleansing and ventilating of schoolrooms have been so long neglected is an additional reason for losing no more time in carrying out the necessary improvements.

I am convinced that many high schools, after having been shown that there are so many sickly children amongst their pupils, will do all in their power to bring about a better state of things; but a complete and comprehensive improvement in the lower schools as well, will not be effected until we obtain legislation commensurate with the needs of the present day. It is very desirable that we, in Denmark, should follow the example of France and Sweden in appointing to all our schools medical officers, whose duty it should be not only to see that hygienic regulations are fully carried out, but to give the masters valuable hints about individual pupils. Only when medical men thus appointed can watch the progress of the different pupils throughout their school career, can absolutely reliable school statistics be gradually collected.

The proposal made by Professor Hornemann in 1860, to keep a record book, in which the health of every pupil should be entered from a medical certificate signed by the family doctor at the beginning of every term, would, if carried out, prove of much value and furnish very instructive information, pending the organisation by law of a more complete system.

After all these revelations it is pretty evident that some medical superintendence for all schools is a necessity, more especially as we do not require of our teachers any, even the most elementary acquaintance with the laws of hygiene.

We have thus no guarantee whatever that the measures which are necessary to the children's physical well-being will be observed. As far as I know, only those ladies who qualify as teachers for the Poor Schools receive any instruction in the principles of hygiene, Professor Hornemann's handbook *On Education,* which they must all read, containing a particularly well-written and concise exposition of the chief physiological processes and their significance, besides the leading rules of school hygiene. Of how much importance he, as a pedagogue, considers it that teachers should have some knowledge of hygienic principles may be gathered from the following extract from his book :—"The ignorance of, and indifference to the nature and functions of the organic life which are commonly found, even in those teachers who are otherwise intelligent and well informed, are no less surprising than deplorable. We make considerable sacrifices to give our children a good education, while at the same time we bestow no thought upon the circumstance that we are sending them to places where, frequently, every breath they take frustrates all our efforts and all our sacrifices.

"The teacher who does not make himself sufficiently acquainted with matters relating to health is responsible for his own ignorance; but what are we to say of those masters who well know the importance to health of fresh air, but who, from carelessness and indifference, omit to air their class-rooms? The time will come, it is to be hoped, when the truth will be much more generally known and recognised by parents, that to inhale carbonic acid is to inhale poison. When that time arrives, the law and the sanitary authorities will also have advanced so far in efficiency that every schoolmaster who does not air his class-rooms several times a day will be called to account for a serious omission of duty; but as the schoolmaster is the self-elected champion of enlightenment, he must not be content to allow himself to be forced onward by the current of public opinion —he must lead the way himself."

It is of the greatest importance for a teacher to know something about the physical development of a child, and the conditions which are necessary to his well-being and proper bodily and mental growth ; and he should also be able to study the

child so as to determine whether periods of slack-
ness in work are due to laziness and inattention
or to physical weakness.   Mistakes in this respect
are common, and may do much harm to the child.
I have known cases of boys being punished almost
daily because they did not write as well as they
used to, when it has turned out that the commencement of St. Vitus's dance or some affection
of the brain was the cause.   It frequently happens
that children who, by reason of a rapid accession
of anæmia or some similar disease, become dull
and slow at their work, are kept in daily, and
have thus some hours of additional work heaped
on to their already crushing burden; such treatment cannot but have a most unfortunate result,
seeing that the children in such cases, above all
things, stand in need of a reduction of work, and
a break in the long school hours.   In these days of
nervousness and relaxed constitutions, cases occur
constantly in which children for a time can hardly
do any work, and have to be taken from school
for several months.   The school might often be
the first to observe the falling off in the child's
capacity for work, and to call the attention of the

parents to the fact; by diminishing the work in·
time it would often be possible to prevent the
disease from developing.

A knowledge of the laws of health should therefore be required of all intending schoolmasters
and mistresses; they should understand clearly
that considerations of the highest importance are
involved, and that they cannot despise or over-
look these if they wish to fulfil in a conscientious
manner their duties as guides and preceptors of
youth.

But when the necessity for medical control is
recognised, it will also be time to grapple much
more energetically than heretofore with another
evil which seems to be gaining ground. I allude
to the numerous so-called private classes here in
town which under that pleasant-sounding but
deceptive appellation elude all official control.
These private classes differ in no way from the
schools; they often force on the children to a
degree that no well-regulated school would
sanction, and the parents congratulate themselves
on the rapidity with which their children learn,
in which they only see a proof of the excellent

system of the private classes without giving a thought to the injury such teaching may cause to the children later on. The rooms of those establishments are usually of the most humble description, and as twenty children are often taught at a time in these small rooms it is difficult to perceive in what respect the form of teaching pursued in them differs from that of the public schools, except that the former, being subject to no control or inspection, can set aside with impunity those considerations to which even the worst public schools must always have a certain amount of regard. A well-regulated public school offers much greater advantages; it has at its disposal superior means of illustration, such as diagrams, maps, etc., which are great helps to instruction, and those private classes which are in a position to afford the same must be exceptionally well placed. In the ones I allude to there are no such aids to teaching, the substitute for them being relentless cramming.

It must be mentioned as an important stride in the matter of hygiene that pupils in whose homes infectious diseases may have arisen are now prohibited from attending school, and it deserves to be specially mentioned that the initiative in this matter was taken by the schools.

Complaint has been made about the length of the consecutive school attendances, and it is certainly very unfortunate that an arrangement such as that now in vogue should ever have been introduced. Six or, as is not unusual, seven hours' work at a stretch, without any long interval, and on some days without even gymnastics, is equally objectionable, whether regarded from a hygienic or a pedagogic standpoint, and a change in this respect is very desirable. I am not aware that this system is allowed in any other country.[1] Having regard, however, to the social and domestic habits which have obtained general acceptance in our capital, it is evident that a complete rearrangement of our school hours would involve many practical difficulties, and that we should therefore ponder well any new proposal lest we lose more in other respects than we gain in the matters of tuition and health. Amongst the better classes the dinner-hour is no longer in the middle of the day, but in

---

[1] In the Danish schools the pupils have six full days' work every week, whole holidays or half-holidays being unknown throughout the school term.—[TRANS.]

the afternoon, usually from four to five o'clock.
If the children were required to return to school
about that time they would have to dine at a
different hour from the rest of the family, which
would be unfortunate in every way. Dinner is,
as a rule, the only substantial meal which children
get, sandwiches otherwise forming the bulk of
their diet; if they were not to dine with the rest
of the family the probability is that they would
not get such a good dinner, not to mention the
inconvenience and in many cases the impossibility
of making two dinners. In addition to this, the
dinner-hour is very often the only time which a
father can spend in the society of his children, and
when his influence and authority are felt; and these
I consider to be so all-important in the training of
children, especially of boys, that everything should
be avoided which might curtail a father's inter-
course with his children, already, in the case of
many business men, so very limited. The school
hours would therefore in any case have to be so
arranged that they could be over before the dinner-
hour, and the evening then left for preparation.
If we could succeed in introducing a more natural

arrangement of the day and begin work earlier, say at seven o'clock in the morning, as in Sweden, much would be already gained. Any changes, however, would have to be carefully thought out before being put into practice. Being compelled, meanwhile, to retain the present most unfortunate system, we must not lose sight of the fact that one long spell of work is far more exhausting to the child than the same number of hours would be if split up by a considerable interval. Besides, when the children are at home all the afternoon, from two or three o'clock, the three or four hours they spend in preparation do not seem to the parents to be much, and it is assuredly owing to this that parents often request the school to give their children more work. If the school hours were divided in a natural and proper manner it would soon be evident to all that the children's time was more than sufficiently taken up, and we should in all probability hear no complaints to the effect that the children lacked occupation.

But if we cannot at present look for any considerable break in the daily school hours, it is, at any rate, absolutely necessary that the children should have a longer play-hour about noon—half an hour at the very least—not only to give them a short rest from work but mainly to allow them sufficient time for lunch. It is strange that the need of this has been so entirely overlooked. Most schools, it is true, allow eight or ten minutes between each class, but this is far too short a time for a boy to eat his lunch in. A meal should be taken at one time, and not in snatches at hourly intervals; this is totally opposed to all physiological teaching, as it weakens the appetite and impairs digestion. It is true that children sometimes make up for the inadequate lunch-time by eating or rather devouring their sandwiches surreptitiously in class, but that this is wrong requires no proof. Many children eat slowly, and if they are interrupted they do not eat any more; it is a common complaint, and one which has been stated in many of my schedules, that as soon as they go back to school the children lose their appetites and bring back half their lunch, while throughout the holidays they eat heartily enough. Very often this is due to the scant time allowed for lunch, but for nervous and anæmic children—and the school

K

must always bear in mind that it has to deal with a large proportion of such—good substantial nourishment is of the highest importance; if their appetite is poor, everything ought to be done to improve it.

I know that the schools will reply to all this, that they cannot give a longer lunch-time without increasing the school hours, but this just shows how forced is the work, and how essential it is that some relief should be obtained.

As an instance of the importance which other countries attach to a proper distribution of school hours, I will give a short report of a discussion in the Swedish Medical Society, Stockholm (*Hygeia*, Sept. and Oct. Nos., 1880). By the Education Act of 1878 it is enacted that in the five youngest classes in all the Swedish High Schools the pupils must not be worked for more than two hours at a time, after which an interval of two hours is enjoined, though half an hour of this may be devoted to singing or gymnastics. This arrangement was introduced because the Swedish pedagogues thought that longer spells of work must fatigue the children. The result of this was that on some days the school hours were divided into three sections, *e.g.* in summer from seven to nine, eleven to one, and three to four. In many places this splitting up of the time proved rather a disadvantage, particularly if any of the pupils lived far from school, but also because the home work was interrupted thereby. Several schools therefore applied for permission to extend the limit to three hours at a time, with an interval of two hours, confining the work, however, as much as possible to the early part of the day. Before granting this request the Government demanded the opinion of the Medical Society, of which the following is a résumé :—" Three hours' consecutive work is permissible if an interval of ten minutes be allowed for every hour, and one hour of the three set apart for easy work, such as singing, writing, or the like. After that there must be two hours' complete rest, not mere nominal rest devoted to singing or gymnastics, partly to allow the children plenty of time for lunch and recreation, partly to admit of the class-rooms being properly ventilated. After these two hours the work should be recommenced, so that

it might be over before the dinner-hour, leaving
the afternoon for preparation."

Such an arrangement appears to entirely correspond with pedagogic and hygienic demands for
a proper distribution of work hours, and its main
features may well be taken by us as a model.
The extreme care with which all such questions
are treated in Sweden, and the fact that no change
is ever made without the opinion of medical men
being taken as to its probable influence on the
health of the children, contrast strongly with our
educational legislation and regulations, which are
committed entirely to the hands of pedagogues,
without any such provision on behalf of the
children's health as consultation with medical
men would ensure. The result is that hygienic
considerations are with us completely overlooked.

Quite as important as the reduction of mental
work is it that the physical development of school
children should be promoted by bodily exercise.
This ought to take a much more prominent place
than it does in the school curriculum, and not
be regarded as less important than any other
branch of instruction. In boys' schools gymnas-

tics are undoubtedly taught more extensively
than they used to be; there are classes in some
schools in which four hours a week are devoted
to gymnastics, but this is far from being the
case throughout, three hours a week being an
exceptional average for any one class of the
aggregated schools. This is not enough; as a
rule one hour's bodily exercise (gymnastics or some
organised game) should be the daily allowance.
I doubt whether the gymnastic training generally
given in schools is properly adapted for children.
The powers of endurance which gymnastics are
intended to call forth in soldiers are not so
necessary in the case of children; with them the
main thing is to strengthen all parts of the body,
especially the muscles of the arms and trunk,
which they have fewer opportunities of exercising,
and which are most apt to become relaxed by the
sedentary work of school. The exercises are
certainly better in many schools than when I was
at school, when the "horse" was the great thing,
while the trapeze, parallel bars, etc., were almost
unknown. These are certainly much better for
schoolboys, the more so as the greater variety in

the exercises, besides being more beneficial to the
body, greatly tends to kindle a useful spirit of
rivalry.   Instead of boring a boy, gymnastics
ought to possess attractions for him, so that he
may be induced to continue the exercises after he
leaves school, as so very rarely happens now.   It
is therefore very desirable for the instructor to
know the right exercises to choose, and to direct
them with life and energy so as to awaken the
zeal of the pupils.   We can hardly expect this
unless the instructor, however splendid a gymnast,
be also specially qualified to teach children.   It
is very characteristic of the want of interest in
bodily exercises existing in Denmark, that out of
the 3141 boys examined by me there were only
86 who had private lessons in gymnastics, riding,
or fencing.   If sufficient energy and zest were
imparted to the instruction at school many more
boys would undoubtedly go in for these exercises
out of school, and in many cases this would be
most beneficial.

Matters are much worse in the girls' schools,
those examined giving an average of one and a
half hour of gymnastics weekly; but in many,

particularly of the smaller schools, these are not taught at all, while in some the instruction is so loosely conducted as to be almost useless. I must add, however, that in other schools again it is really a pleasure to see how well the girls go through their exercises, and with what evident relish. They only lack opportunities; the taste for bodily exercise is, I think, quite as great with girls as with boys, and the need of it is often much greater. It would be a real blessing if these nervous and anæmic girls could daily exchange an hour of reading or music for one of gymnastics, properly directed, and adapted to their strength and sex. I have often had opportunities of convincing myself of the healthy effect of such exercise upon the whole development, carriage, and motions of young girls. The rank which gymnastics now take in girls' schools is quite disproportionate to their value as compared with any other pursuits, but the instruction in them must be thorough, efficient, and energetic; in many schools they are taught in a most desultory manner, and can hardly be said to be more than tolerated, whereas their proper place is among the chief subjects.

The same writer who has denounced long consecutive school hours says : " Give boys back their games; let them romp for an hour or two every day. . . . What benefit can a boy derive from a forced and formal constitutional walk, which, during the greater part of the year, has to be taken in the darker hours of the day ?   A man, who feels that it is good for him to walk deliberately, can do so, but for a boy, the exercise he takes ought to contain an element of pleasure and amusement; he will not exert himself unless he is thoroughly animated or sees something to be gained thereby. Games afford both exercise and enjoyment, and in these his natural predilection for associating with boys of his own age is indulged.   Once more, then, I say, ' Give schoolboys their games again.'"

The above quotation undoubtedly touches one of the most universally felt wants in our system of training, viz. the absence of facilities for children to romp and play in a natural way ; if they are deprived of these they soon cease to be boys, and too early regard themselves as men, and consequently above all childish pastimes, amongst which they include gymnastics and physical exercises.

In this they are not infrequently encouraged by unwise parents, who feel flattered at seeing their sons so early developed into sedate and reflective beings, as they fondly imagine. But if we are to hope for success in our efforts to make the present race healthier and stronger, we must not expect that the reformation of the school system alone is to accomplish it. The out-of-school training must also be carried on in a rational and suitable manner, otherwise the result will be a meagre one. In this respect there are many prejudices and mistaken ideas to be overcome. I have heard even highly cultivated and intelligent men remark: "Let boys have plenty to do at school, or else they will spend their time in reading unwholesome literature, which is pernicious to them." True, if this really would be the necessary result of more leisure; but does not this seem rather a weak admission on the part of parents that they do not know how to awaken their children's interest for improving literature, or to aid and encourage them in private study, according to their different tastes? And is it not very characteristic evidence of the fact that besides reading they know of no other employment for their children's time? When children have their nine hours' work a day it is not reading they should have in the scrap of waking life that remains to them; they require physical occupation. Encourage them in winter to go in for gymnastics, shooting, skating, etc.; let them learn a little of some useful handicraft—in short, let them take up anything that exercises and employs their physical powers, and then at night they will be more inclined to go early to bed than to sit up reading rubbish or worse.

On the other hand, when the days are longer, it would be a great boon if such games as football, cricket, and tennis were played in our country as in England and Sweden; they form a necessary complement to gymnastics, and may indeed often partly supersede them. Without games it is scarcely possible to call forth children's interest for all sorts of physical pursuits; the long, sedentary school work makes them, in the older classes, languid, lazy, and averse to the exercise of which they stand in so great need. If they are not habituated to, and trained in manly sports when quite young they will hardly be induced to take them up as they grow older. Well-organised games under the supervision of the masters tend also to promote good discipline—upon which latter point some of our schools have no reason to pride themselves.

There is a great dearth in Copenhagen of good well-fitted-up gymnasia, which might be used both by boys' and girls' schools, and, after school hours, by other children as well. The only large gymnasium in the town is very defective; the floor is of concrete, the place cannot be heated up in winter, and it is altogether so cheerless that, as proved sufficiently by experience, it rather repels than attracts the young. There is so little taste for physical exercise amongst us, and so little is done to stimulate it, that if we would not sink into a state of utter lassitude and effeminacy we must make earnest and constant efforts not only to convince the young of the necessity of developing their muscular framework but to supply them with the means of doing so.

Let children be allowed to romp and play in the open air as much as possible, and do not send

the young ones at the early age of five to stuffy
private schools in order to get rid of them at
home. The custom of sending infants to school
before their faculty for assimilating knowledge
has appeared, has done a great deal of harm, and
many schools complain of this. Lessons ought
not, as a rule, to be begun before the age of six or
seven. The age-columns in Table V. show that
in all classes there are boys who are two or three
years too young for their respective classes, and
who thus are forced beyond their natural stages of
development, which, of course, can only be injurious
to them.

Later on, when the real work of school begins,
in the shape of home preparation and exercises, it
is still more necessary for parents to be on their
guard. There are children who, as we have seen,
at the age of nine have to work ten hours a day
or more, including music lessons. This is not
altogether the fault of the school; it is the duty
of the parents to carefully observe how long the
child works, and, particularly if he is weak and
sickly, to avoid all forcing or superfluous toil.
Schools are constantly complaining that many

parents try to force their children far beyond their strength and capacity, and reproach the school into the bargain for not teaching them enough. False ambition often induces parents, against the advice of the school, to keep boys at their studies who would be far better and healthier at some practical work. Thus parents, though they may make great personal and pecuniary sacrifices to bring them on, are often to blame for the children not being rightly and properly developed. This will continue to be the case until it be more widely recognised that knowledge is not the only thing we must give our children, but that a healthy frame, a strong and resolute character, are equally if not more necessary to the young who have to go out into the world and make a way for themselves. Knowledge is a thing which they can to a great extent acquire later on, if they possess energy and endurance; but a delicate frame and a feeble character will hamper and depress them in every relation of life.

As for girls, regular constant participation in household duties is both a useful and a healthy occupation; this, instead of the excessive amount of study between the ages of thirteen to sixteen, together with a few hours daily at school, would help to fill up their time in a much more natural manner, and, along with gymnastics, which is as necessary for girls as for boys, would give them the physical exercise which they now lack. Many a young wife must often have regretted that her mother did not instruct her in any of those matters so necessary to make a home comfortable, and for which she now has to pay dearly in experience. Unless her school education be discontinued at an unnaturally early stage, her mental and physical powers will in this manner be much more effect-ually strengthened and developed. Only, be it re-membered, if a girl is to derive any real advantage from this work she must apply herself to it with as much diligence as to any other kind of study.

In our capital there is another factor which often works much mischief, viz. that many children are too early and too frequently allowed to go out to parties. All teachers, both in boys' and girls' schools, are loud and unanimous in their com-plaints that children often come to school unpre-pared and knocked up, or remain away altogether, because their parents have allowed them to participate in all sorts of gaiety and amusements. This, of course, is bound to have a bad effect both upon work and health. Children who go to school, and from whom a considerable amount of daily work is required, must live regularly and go to bed at proper hours, so that they may be fresh for their tasks, otherwise they get little good from the teaching ; if they repeatedly come to school tired and worn out they lose all relish and capacity for work, besides becoming nervous and fretful from want of sleep.

Besides those children who more or less exceptionally sit up late at night there are, as I have shown before, no less than 8 per cent of the total number of children who may be said as a rule to get too little sleep. Here, again, it is the duty of the parents to see that the children conform to sound physiological rules; if this be neglected, the children will suffer in the long run. It is most often the elder pupils who sit up late at night, and as the reading of unwholesome books, which many are justly afraid of, most often goes on at that time, it would be doubly well if parents always saw that their children went to bed at a proper hour, and of course did not continue their reading there.

In my opinion it is a great mistake in our system of education that our chief endeavours have been so exclusively directed towards teaching as many different subjects as possible. It is undoubtedly a very good thing to possess varied acquirements, but it is necessary to know how to make use of them, otherwise they are a dead weight on the mind of the possessor. With fewer mental attainments, but with a thorough grasp of what he knows, a strong and healthy man will accomplish far more than will one who, with perhaps more numerous acquisitions, is nevertheless, owing to his weaker character and will, anxious and over-cautious, fearful of all responsibility, and unable consequently to prosecute anything with vigour and energy. As the training of the young is at present carried on with us, soft and flaccid characters are likely to be developed, but it is not such this age requires; it demands strong and hardy natures, for it uses roughly those who have to make their own way in life.

To expect everything from a reformation of school training would only lead to disappointment; the home and the school must work hand in hand and assist each other. Then, and only then, will a truly satisfactory result be attained. It will require a vast amount of persevering attention, and not least on the part of those who, as schoolmasters and mistresses, are specially charged with the guidance and development of the coming race, to secure the abolition of educational overpressure and its attendant evils.

It has not been my intention in this work to produce complete and exhaustive statistics of all the higher boys' schools in Denmark. My inquiry only embraces the boys' and girls' high schools in Copenhagen. It is possible that a better state of things exists outside our capital; at all events the children in our villages and small provincial towns have the great advantage of being able to romp and run about with much greater freedom than the Copenhagen children. Perfectly reliable statistics can of course only be obtained by means of extensive and repeated investigations; I have merely taken the first step. Here, for the first time, has proof been adduced to show how great is the sickliness in our schools, and how long are the work hours; both these conditions were hitherto unknown. New inquiries must be set on foot, and these will, I am sure, go to prove that in the main my results are correct; but we have already obtained enough upon which to base a profitable discussion, and as a contribution to this I beg that the latter half of this work be regarded. Although much of it has been said by others in various papers and periodicals I have deemed it advisable to collect it all here.

On the subject of the lower class schools we have as yet absolutely no information of the kind.

In No. 213 of *Berling's Gazette*, 1880, I took the liberty of urging the Government to appoint a commission, consisting of pedagogues, doctors, architects, and other professional men, to institute a minute inquiry into the state of our schools, with a view to making some proposals as to the best means of improving their hygienic condition. I now make free again to urge that this be done.

Not until Government takes the matter up will

it be possible to collect the mass of information necessary for a complete solution of the questions connected with this subject. My contributions have only thrown light on a few points, but the results have been such, I think, as to show the necessity of a complete and comprehensive inquiry.

NOTE.—Since the publication of Dr. Hertel's report a Government Commission, composed of public officials, teachers, and physicians, has held an inquiry into the state of health of Danish school children, and has fully confirmed the conclusions at which he arrived. The Commission included in its investigation schools of all grades, and collected exact information respecting the health state of 28,225 children, 16,889 boys and 11,225 girls. Of the boys 29 per cent and of the girls 41 per cent are, the Commission declares, in a sickly state of health. It will be recollected that Dr. Hertel's percentages of sickly were 31 for boys and 39 for girls. The Commission finds, as Dr. Hertel did, that anæmia, scrofula, and headaches are the most prevalent complaints amongst school children. As regards failure of eyesight in the young in Denmark the Commission makes some startling revelations. It ascertained by special examination that in the classical department of the largest schools in Copenhagen cases of shortsightedness occur amongst the boys in the different classes in the following proportions :—

No. of Class	I.	II.	III.	IV.	V.	VI.
Percentage of short-sighted boys	14·7	15·1	29·6	27·2	38·3	45·5

Denmark, in its disregard of natural laws, is evidently fast approaching the plight of the nation mentioned by Ezekiel, " which have eyes to see and see not ; they have ears to hear and hear not, for they are a rebellious house."

1 *Healthy* ——— *Mixed & Classical* — — *Modern* 2 *Sickly* ——— *Mixed & Classical* ——-*Modern* 3 *Non returned* ══ *Mixed & Classical* ——-*Modern*

———————	*Mixed & Classical (Rhetorical sect)*
··················	*Preparatory schools*
—·—·—·—·—	*Classical (Natural science sect.)*
— — — — —	*Modern*

CHART IV.

HOURS OF WORK *per diem*—GIRLS' SCHOOLS.

Lightning Source UK Ltd.
Milton Keynes UK
UKHW020647241218
334505UK00007B/124/P